A PARADOXICAL ALLIANCE

An Anglo-American Analysis of The Left's Love
Affair with Islam

Cover art by Martina Markota and Lucy Brown.

With special thanks to Dr. John Press and James Linton.

Contents

Foreword: by Paul Weston

This book by Jack Buckby and Matt Palumbo is long overdue. Britain and the West finds itself in a very precarious position as we look to the third decade of the 21st century. We pride ourselves on values which we claim are representative of Western civilisation, but sadly, these values have little to do with the founding principles of the West and a great deal to do with facilitating the demise of the West.

Whenever one of our politicians talks about British values, they are always presented through the prism of politically correct thought toward anything and everything but the British as a people and a culture. Take for example the much-parroted British value of tolerance. Britain was forged on Judeo-Christian, Greco-Roman tradition, not tolerance. And tolerance will not extend our heritage, our traditions, our culture or indeed the British people themselves.

We are now being asked to tolerate the intolerant. Specifically, the mono-cultural and supremacist religious and political ideology of Islam, coupled also with the aggressive and destructive Leftist ideology which has never looked with favour upon the Christian, capitalist underpinnings of our society which made us so resistant to Socialist revolution.

This Leftist/Islamic Alliance now poses a threat to Britain and the West in the 21st century as serious and as potentially destructive as the 20th century threats of Nazism and Communism. The astonishing thing about our dire situation is the endless reluctance to confront what needs to be confronted if we are to leave a peaceful, stable and prosperous society to our children and grandchildren.

This book does indeed confront the issues. It tells us the truth about the violent and supremacist ideology of Islam. It also details the advances made by radicals posing as moderates within our political world. Buckby and Palumbo talk of the ever-growing power of the Muslim vote, which comes naturally with their ever growing demographic.

Various Muslim organisations are identified and exposed as radical despite the moderate fronts they promote to the curiously disinterested mainstream investigative media. This book highlights the shady and shocking relationship between Islamic movements and senior members (both past and present) of the British Labour Party.

Britain is heading toward an unimaginable future. I liken it to a locomotive speeding toward the cliff edge. The driver refuses to brake and stop. The passengers are blissfully unaware of their terminal destination. Some brave souls are risking life and limb as they try to clamber aboard in order to halt the train, but their feeble efforts are no match for the on-board defences made up of machine guns manned by actors, teachers, senior policemen, judges and of course the BBC, whose withering arc of fire cuts down each and every man and woman long before they could even get a toehold on the rapidly accelerating mass of metal hurtling toward the abyss.

This book is a step toward gaining that necessary toehold. People need to read and understand the potential catastrophe that awaits us. We are living in Orwellian times where up is down and down is up, a state of mind reinforced by repetitive propaganda doled out by all those who control the means of education and the means of information. To paraphrase George Orwell, Islam is peace, Freedom is slavery, Ignorance is strength.

I hope many people read this book by Mr. Buckby and Mr. Palumbo, and that they absorb and understand what is being said. There are many who wish to remain willfully ignorant about the most pressing issue of the 21st century, but for those who are more open-minded I would encourage them to refute the idea that Ignorance is strength and that Islam is peace. Reality and honesty must replace the fantasy and lies perpetuated by the Leftist/Islamic Alliance. So don't just read this book, buy five more and send them to your friends – even if it means one or two might never call you up again!

BRITAIN

Introduction

In 1337, Edward III of England refused to pay homage to Philip VI of France. Shakespeare's Henry V, border changes (namely the confiscation of English land in Aquitaine, including Gascony), and the 100 Years War resulted. Throughout history, Europe has seen hundreds of alliances, treaties and agreements that have had implications ranging from war and oppression to freedom, border changes and cultural shifts. Such huge changes, however, do not always require direct actions from world leaders. The consequences of our modern threat, the Paradoxical Alliance, could be as severe as any in history.

The alliance we face today comes in the form of mutual efforts from multiculturalists and Islam. This is an alliance so dangerous that it could result in the collapse of many parts of Western society. And, unlike with the 100 Years War, thousands of years' worth of thinking, action and ideological evolution that have made our modern Western world, the most scientific, advanced, wealthy, and successful civilisation to have ever existed, have been systematically dismantled within a matter of 50 years or fewer.

The Second World War killed more than 60 million people, and it's not inconceivable to suggest this kind of figure can be killed again. How? Through Islamisation: the invitation of encroaching Islamic ideals, all aiming to establish Islamic rule in Europe. Since the birth of Islam, we have seen the death of 120 million Africans, 60 million Christians, 80 million Hindus, and 10 million Buddhists. All this has come from attempts to establish Islamic theocratic rule. Islam, in fact means submission - and who has invited this program of submission into the West? The multicultural Left.

One would assume that any freedom loving Westerner would be appalled at such numbers and the increasing presence of Sharia and Islam, generally, across the West. It appears however that the politically neutral population of Britain are often scared to talk about this issue. They are cowed by the multicultural Left calling them racist. Worse yet, the multicultural left's attacks come physically and verbally – from individuals - or through penalties including imprisonment or losing of one's job- via institutions. Naturally, the Left's working in favour of Islam has attracted the attention of Muslims and Sharia fanatics throughout the West, and now we see a truly terrifying and Paradoxical Alliance that is supporting bloodshed, violence, and oppression in the greatest civilisation on Earth.

My own case illustrates the mechanisms of this alliance. In 2012, I attempted to start a student society at the University of Liverpool, which was designed to inform students of the dangers of Islam, and group likeminded young political thinkers together. We used the word 'culturist' to indicate that we were concerned with the impact of cultural diversity; we were not racist. Very quickly, we became targeted by the significant presence of the Left at university - we were physically harassed and threatened by other students and ironically named antifascist organisations operating in the city. But instead of investigating them, the university came after me. Eventually I was removed from the university in what was clearly a politically-motivated attack. This egregious example is symptomatic of the pressures exerted by professors, employers, government, and media across all British institutions.

The Paradoxical Alliance is paradoxical because under the Sharia law that the multicultural left champion, the Left would be subjugated, demonised and killed. But in order to claim moral high ground and justify their purging in universities of those who dissent from their ideological line, the Left has perverted language and reversed meanings with thoroughness that would amaze those living in George Orwell's 1984. To combat this perversion of language, this book will prove how those of us who oppose the multicultural left - we conservative culturists - are really the ones who stand for individual freedoms, responsibility and cultural diversity. We must point out the illogical and dangerous nature of the Paradoxical Alliance.

In order to unravel the Paradoxical Alliance, and in order to point out exactly where and how we need to inject some culturist truth serum, this book will detail the very mechanisms in the very institutions, that give the Paradoxical Alliance its strength; education and policing; politics via pressure groups; and our lack of responses to terrorism. The British are some of the worst affected people across Europe when it comes to liberal bias and encroaching Islamic fascism. As such, in looking at how these mechanisms give the Paradoxical Alliance so much power in Britain, it will also show other western nations what they can expect to see in coming years. Additionally, this book will provide a powerful antidote that can be applied in America, continental Europe, and the West more broadly.

Context

This book is split into two sections. The first half will explore the Paradoxical Alliance between the Left and Islam in the United Kingdom. In this section, the term 'Left' or 'Leftists' will be used interchangeably with 'Multiculturalists'. This will refer not only to socially and politically left-wing organisations, parties, think tanks and charities, but also to so-called 'conservative' organisations, parties, think tanks and charities that are complicit in the multicultural restructuring of Britain's institutions and society.

Any first-person references in the first half of the book will refer to the experiences of this writer, Jack Buckby.

The second half of this book will look at these same issues in the United States, through the experiences and observations of A Paradoxical Alliance co-author Matt Palumbo. Matt reserves the right to use American English, because, in his words, "we won the war."

CHAPTER ONE
Multiculturalism and Islam: The Actors in the Paradoxical Alliance

The Nature of Multiculturalism

Multiculturalism seeks to unite the increasingly diverse western nations by "celebrating diversity." This laudable goal ultimately seeks to prevent the horrors resulting from Nazi Germany's racial intolerance. Multiculturalism ideologues start by noting that our western nations are diverse. Then they hope that we can create harmony out of diversity by accepting, tolerating and even celebrating the diversity that unites us. They consider not celebrating such diversity as dangerous. "It can disunite us and even lead to genocide", they warn us. Whist their intentions are good, their shrill rhetoric confusing race and culture, and falsification, has led them to partner with a theocratic system that would undermine the very liberal values they seek to protect. Ironically, one giant error committed by multiculturalists is to completely ignore the reality of cultural diversity.

Take Islam, for example: There have been more than 66,000 cases of women and young girls in Britain subjected to female genital mutilation, according to a government-funded study by 'Forward.' This study has since been deleted from their website. A 2012 BBC poll showed that two thirds of young British Muslims are in favour of honour killings and violence against those who dishonour their families. Seventy-eight percent of British Muslims support the punishment of those who publish cartoons that mock the Prophet Muhammad. One in three British Muslims between the ages of sixteen and twenty-four believe that those who leave the Islamic faith (apostates) should be killed. And, in

2009, a Gallup survey couldn't find a single British Muslim that approved of homosexuality.

When you ask a multiculturalist if they support female genital mutilation the paradox becomes apparent. They do not. They will then attempt to reduce their cognitive dissonance by telling you that Islam has nothing to do with that barbarous practice. This leads to a nearly schizophrenic impasse whereby they constantly tell people what is and is not real Islam. We will look into the nature of 'real Islam' later – but the point is that they cannot accept that cultural diversity is real. Accepting this would mean they have to admit that multiculturalism asks us to celebrate some pretty nasty cultural practices and attitudes.

Usually, multiculturalists do not want to face the existence or nature of cultural diversity which, paradoxically, they support. So rather than discuss the issues involved, the complications diversity brings, value assertions and such topics, they attempt to silence the very discussion underway; doing this by calling anyone who points out the negative aspects of cultural diversity 'racist.' Typically, they'll hark back to WWII and associate their interlocutor with the mad, genocidal intentions of Adolph Hitler by virtuously declaring that promoting his genocidal race hatred is outside the boundaries of acceptable conversation.

The persistent claims by multiculturalists that anybody who discusses the reality or potential negative aspects of cultural diversity is a 'racist' would not be so dangerous were we simply discussing private conversations. But this tactic has been used to silence all forms of dissent in universities, media, and politics. Thus before one becomes a teacher or a politician, one must swear allegiance to multiculturalism and its celebration (and implied absence of criticism) of all cultures – especially Islam. The media destroys the lives of all who would fail to celebrate Islam. While their goals may be liberal, the results squash freedom of speech at a societal level. Ultimately, this inability to discuss the true nature of Islam could lead to the downfall of Britain as we know it.

Muhammad's Life Story

To understand the Paradoxical Alliance, we must understand Islam, and this starts with understanding the prophet Muhammad. When, like Pavlov's dogs, multiculturalists repeat that "Islam is a religion of peace" after each new terrorist act, they are making a statement against diversity. They are implicitly reinforcing the idea that all religions are one, all have the same core values, and all, ultimately, celebrate love and compassion. They are also making an incorrect statement: that "Islam abhors violence." The easiest way to refute these falsehoods is to review the life of Islam's only prophet, Muhammad.

Muhammad was born in 570 AD in what is now Saudi Arabia. As a child, he lived with several family members and we hear nothing else about him until at the age of twenty-five when he marries his wealthy cousin, Kadijah. He experienced his first religious vision at the age of 40, and three years later, in 613 AD, he began to preach Islam publicly in Mecca. There he attacked the indigenous Meccan polytheism enshrined in the large black box that Muslims now visit annually, the Kabaa. His recruitment efforts, however, largely fell on deaf ears causing him to move on, geographically and ideologically.

In the year 622 Muhammad moved from Mecca to Medina. This is a very important milestone in Islamic history and is known as Hijra. The event marks the year zero in

Islamic calendars. It also marks Muhammad's transition from a preacher to that of a military and political leader. With his change to more violent and oppressive tactics in Medina, Muhammad began to have remarkable success, becoming both the religious and the political leader of the city.

In 620 Muhammad's first wife died. A month later he married another woman, Sawda bint Zam'a, though with limited rights for her. In the year 623, Muhammad consummated his marriage to his nine-year-old bride, Aisha, when he was in his early fifties. On two occasions, he forcibly took war captives (whose husbands he had first slaughtered/beheaded) and married them that same day. Those victims were named Safiyah and Juwairiyah. Muhammad officially had twelve wives during his lifetime and nine when he died. They ranged in age from nine to forty years old. He also had many unofficial 'brides' (the institution then not being what it is now) and enjoyed the company of numerous concubines.

In Medina, Muhammad ruled with violence. In one especially notorious incident in 627, a Jewish tribe had not sided with Mohammed against the Meccans, and had possibly given the latter material aid. Muhammad's forces besieged them for 25 days until they surrendered. A judge gave a verdict that the men who had reached puberty be killed and the women and children taken as captive. Agreeing, Muhammad told the judge, "You have given the judgment of Allah above the seven heavens." With Mohammed's acquiescence, 600 – 900 Jews were beheaded.

Muhammad's attacks were not limited to Medina. The first attack on Mecca was launched in 624 during a holy month when fighting was prohibited. In this attack, he took seventy hostages for ransom. In the subsequent raid, he had a critic beheaded and another twenty-four thrown in a well. He was injured in one battle but kept on fighting. In 629 he launched his first raid into Christian lands. In one glorious victory, he captured 6,000 women and children and consolidated most of the Arabian Peninsula under Islam. All totalled, Muhammad personally engaged in over twenty significant battles. Muhammad spent his final days with his now eighteen-year-old child bride, Aisha, and finally died in 632.

Basic Facts

Some might protest that the words above contain grievous slander, particularly the parts that implicate him in pederasty and polygamy. They might say that this outline of his life – including the beheading story – goes out of the way to portray him as a violent warlord.

However, nothing written above is conjecture. It does not rely on obscure theological doctrine - it is all agreed upon fact. No Muslim scholar or lay historian would dispute the accuracy of the timeline and facts above. Furthermore, Muhammad lived well within historical times of a literate people. Whereas facts about Jesus's life are murky, facts about Mohammed's life are well documented by various contemporary sources. The above is not slander - it is fact acknowledged by all Muslims and historians.

Muhammad lived in violent times when tribes were constantly battling, and so he ruled in the only way possible. But, it is completely inaccurate to say that Mohammed was not violent when he was involved with violent attacks on a regular basis. It is completely factually inaccurate to say that he opposed beheading (he sanctioned it). It is completely inaccurate to say that Muhammad promoted marriage concepts compatible with those of Western ideals (he had a nine-year-old bride and nine wives simultaneously).

When confronted with the biographical timeline above, multiculturalists routinely, and paradoxically, remind you that Christianity has been violent too. This is paradoxical because these very same multiculturalists who 'celebrate diversity' are feverishly working to establish that no diversity exists. Still, they are correct - Christian history has been violent. The difference however is that violence in Christianity comes from contradicting the example of Jesus, whereas Muslim violence comes from faithfully following their prophet's example. Mohammad would've stoned to death the prostitutes that Jesus associated with.

Remember that when the Roman's captured Jesus, Simon Peter retaliated by grabbing a sword and cutting off his ear. Jesus then said, "Put up again thy sword into his place: for all they that take the sword shall perish with the sword." However one interprets this, Jesus denounced violence. There is no doubt that Mohammed would not have given up without a battle. Diversity exists.

It is understandable that western leaders want to forestall the potential communal violence that lays inchoate in multicultural societies by calling Islam, "the religion of peace." But, it is also without any foundation in Mohammed's actions. Islam was founded and spread by the sword and, as Sun Tzu would tell you, it is dangerous to underestimate your enemy. Make no mistake, Muhammad's example to his followers was one of nearly unrelenting violence. So how can anyone in their right mind say that Islam might be a religion of peace? We'll now look at abstract theological basis of this claim.

Abrogation

Early in his career, when Muhammad was in Mecca and greatly outnumbered, he promulgated some peaceful-sounding ideas. For example, he said "there is no compulsion in religion." But, upon entering Medina and forming an army, he changed his tune and tactics entirely. After entering Medina, he consistently called for and enacted violent suppression against enemies and infidels.

Qur'anic suras are not chronological. The suras (or chapters) are arranged by length and not chronologically in the time they were written. The longest sura is at the beginning and the shortest at the end. This means that readers are unable to follow it logically or decide the structure of events within the book. The concept of abrogation is essentially the nullification, the voiding of earlier, friendly passages that were designed to entice the Jews and Christians to follow the new doctrine.

After Muhammad's ideas were rejected, these earlier verses became redundant, and suras began to contradict one another. A prime example can be found at 29:46:

> And dispute ye not with the People of the Book, except with means better (than mere disputation), unless it be with those of them who inflict wrong (and injury): but say, 'We believe in the revelation which has come down to us and in that which came down to you; Our Allah and your Allah is one.

This is superseded by 9:29:

> Fight those who believe not in Allah, nor the Last Day, nor hold that forbidden which hath been forbidden by Allah and His Messenger, nor

acknowledge the religion of Truth (even if they are) of the People of the Book, until they pay the Jizya with willing submission, and feel themselves subdued.

Abrogation is necessary to make the Qur'an logical. Without it the book is not coherent or rational with regards to message or order.

The nature of the Qur'an, and Muhammad's doctrine, changed. Perhaps if Jews and Christians hadn't rejected his supremacist doctrine, then these peaceful verses would be dominant (assuming that Muhammad was just making this all up as he went along – which is almost certainly the case), and it would be factually correct to suggest they still represent Islam – but they simply don't. In fact, abrogation is confirmed in sura 2:106:

If we abrogate a verse or cause it to be forgotten, we will replace it by a better one or similar. Did you not know that it is God who has sovereignty over the heavens and the earth, and that there is none besides Him to protect or help you?

The very existence of the Medina phase of Muhammad's life proves the existence of abrogation along, of course, with the explicit references within the Qur'an itself. This is the nullification of previous 'ideals' in favour of supremacist, warmongering, totalitarian, vicious, violent practices, beliefs and demands. All references to Jihad, after all, come from the Medina phase.

Abrogation is widely ignored in the Western world, both by Muslims and non-Muslims. If it weren't, then those under threat would understand the nature of Islam. Instead, the West is taught by governments, schools and institutions that Islam is a religion of peace, and that we must be tolerant

15

and loving to the constantly increasing number of Muslims in our communities.

Further confusion about the nature of Islam comes from the practice of Taqiyya. Allah is the great deceiver (Qur'an 3:54, 8:30), and his followers use Taqiyya to fool the disbelievers. The primary method of deceit is through the order of the Qur'an, which leads readers to assume that the violent and peaceful verses are scattered randomly throughout the text, and that Allah is purposely confusing so that the text can be 'interpreted.' The vast majority of verses in the Muslim holy book refer to jihad of some form. Obscuring abrogation, Taqiyya is just a logical extension of that doctrine.

All Islamic theologians affirm the principle of abrogation. Even if we were to take this to be disputed obscure doctrine, the delusions of Leftists about the reality of Islam can be proven wrong with obvious, accessible facts about Muhammad's life. In keeping with the basic outline of Muhammad's life, our daily news clearly depicts violent footage of infidels being killed in the name of Muhammad. And as they are performing their heinous acts, these jihadists often treat us to the chapter and verse justifications for their actions.

Indeed, this was the case with the killing of Lee Rigby, as outlined in Chapter Four. After the British soldier was killed, one of his assailants, Michael Adebolajo, waved his bloody machete and talked to passers-by about why he killed him. Adebolajo said, "There are many, many ayah (sayings) throughout the Qur'an that says we must fight them as they fight us, an eye for an eye and a tooth for a tooth."

Furthermore, both of Rigby's killers, Michael Adebowale and Michael Adebolajo, told the courts that they killed in the name of Islam. The judge in the Lee Rigby trial, Mr. Sweeney, as a multicultural representative of the Paradoxical Alliance, claimed that their actions were, "a betrayal of Islam." In response Adebowale shouted, "That is a lie…you know nothing about Islam!"

Indeed, Adebowale had ample verses to cite. Those who might engage in theological debate over the fact might find another verse. In doing so, they would be showing their ignorance of abrogation. But, beyond theological debate, they would be showing ignorance of the basic facts of Muhammad's life.

The Ultimate Goals of the Paradoxical Alliance

In 1996 Osama Bin Laden issued a fatwa against the United States and claimed that a revival of Islam is beginning all over the world.[1]

It is no secret that Islam's ultimate goal is world domination and that so-called 'extremists' outline perfectly what the Qur'an means and says. In sura 61:9, it is explained to the reader that Allah intends for his message to be spread over the world, becoming victorious over the Mushrikûn, the disbelievers.

61:9 "He it is Who has sent His Messenger (Muhammad) with guidance and the religion of truth (Islamic monotheism) to make it victorious over all (other) religions even though the Mushrikûn (polytheists, pagans, idolaters, and

---

[1] Tristam, Pierre, "Text of Bin Laden's 1996 Declaration of Jihad Against the United States," About News,
http://middleeast.about.com/od/terrorism/a/bin-laden-jihad.htm

disbelievers in the Oneness of Allah and His Messenger Muhammad) hate (it)."[2]

Islam is growing in size, but also increasing its influence through similar methods as used by multiculturalists over the last fifty years. A particularly notable case is known as Operation Trojan Horse. In 2014, the Conservative/Liberal Democrat coalition government announced, in what could be described as an attempt to win back true conservative voters, that schools would now be legally required to teach British values. The announcement came after groups and individuals had been uncovered as attempting to infiltrate the British education system, turning Birmingham schools into Muslim 'training academies' in an attempt to radicalise British youth and further push the violent Islamic agenda on the growing population of children born to Muslim families. This kind of action is nothing less than demanded by Islam.[3]

This is only the beginning, however. The Qur'an teaches its followers to kill all disbelievers where they find them (Qur'an 2:191-193), and fight in the cause of Allah (Qur'an 2:244). This is little more than the preparation of foot soldiers for conflict that will come in the future.

Professional Political Appeasers

The Paradoxical Alliance I describe, that poses a threat to Western and Christian freedoms in Britain, is a combined effort of multiculturalist political parties, pressure groups and Islamic groups. I will use the term 'multiculturalists' throughout this book to describe a

---

[2] Hilali and Khan, *The Noble Qur'an, Riyadh: Darussalam, 1996*
[3] Gilligan, Andrew, "Muslim Extremists, and a Worrying Lesson for Us All," 16th March 2014,
http://www.telegraph.co.uk/education/10700041/Muslim-extremists-and-a-worrying-lesson-for-us-all.html

substantial range of parties, groups and lines of thinking that oppose traditional Christian values, push the 'progressive' view of egalitarianism and the redefinition of traditional institutions, and which are as a result suggesting that Britain and the West are culturally neutral.

In order to fully understand the threat and the actors in the Paradoxical Alliance, it is essential to understand the main political parties and groups in Britain, their aims and what they do to push the multicultural agenda.

Britain has two major parties that would be described as left-wing, and as a result the most prominent proponents of multiculturalism – the Labour Party and the Liberal Democrats. The Labour Party, a socialist political party, is one of the newer political parties in the UK to have ever held power. Established in 1900, the party emerged as a result of the growth of the trade union movement, and quickly grew larger and more powerful than the Liberal Party, a much older party that was founded in 1859.

The Liberal Democrats, which made history by entering into a coalition government with David Cameron's Conservative Party in 2010 – the first in 36 years, was formed out of the old Liberal Party which had been pushed into irrelevance by the growing socialist Labour Party.

Both parties identify as socially liberal, and the Labour Party proudly boasts of its 'positive discrimination' on its website. The official party site reads:

The Labour Party is committed to increasing the representation of women and under-represented groups in Parliament...and proud of our action to tackle the under-representation of women in parliament, including changing

19

the law to allow political parties to use All-Women shortlists to select parliamentary candidates.[4]

So-called 'positive discrimination' is a common trait of the Left and multiculturalists in that these groups attempt to increase the influence and presence of foreign and often incompatible ideas. Harriet Harman, a leading figure in the Labour Party, is known for her extensive work in the cause of 'equality,' having been a major player in the introduction of the Equality Act 2010. The Act, aimed at "reforming and harmonising equality law,"[5] codifies multiple laws, including the Race Relations Act 1976 and the Equal Pay Act 1970, amongst others. At face value, it appears hard to disagree with – the fair treatment of workers is essential for any modern, civilised society. But when one looks deeper into the Act, it reveals itself as a truly discriminatory piece of legislation.

The Equality Act allows employers to purposefully hire candidates who are considered to be a part of 'under-represented groups', meaning that white, straight males can now legally be discriminated against in employment.[6] In turn, this behaviour establishes outside groups more firmly in British institutions, allowing for the increased normalisation of the flawed idea of multiculturalism.

This kind of behaviour is naturally expected of the Left. But what American readers may be surprised to learn

---

[4] Labour Party official website, http://www.labour.org.uk/promoting-diversity
[5] White, Matthew, "The Equality Act 2010," St John's Chambers, 26th August 2010, http://www.stjohnschambers.co.uk/dashboard/wp-content/uploads/2012/07/The-Equality-Act-2010-and-roadmap.pdf
[6] Peacock, Louisa, "Equality Act explained: positive discrimination verses positive action," The Telegraph, 2nd December 2010, http://www.telegraph.co.uk/finance/jobs/8177447/Equality-Act-explained-positive-discrimination-versus-positive-action.html

is that the Conservative Party is guilty of the same kind of Leftist, manipulative discrimination. David Cameron, former Conservative Party leader and Prime Minister, suggested that there are "too many white Christian faces in Britain" and "not enough Muslims."

These are clear examples of how the three main parties in Britain indirectly support multiculturalism – they abuse their power and influence to implement systems that further their political ideology. Indirect action allows them to change Britain gradually without the masses realising exactly what their agenda is. These tactics will be further explored throughout this book – but one thing that is evident is that the main politicians, including so-called conservatives, are hell bent on changing the nature of our society, not only through the Paradoxical Alliance with Islam, but also through successive policies designed to forcefully change society and carefully craft a future population of voters who don't ask questions.

The Labour Party, Conservative Party and Liberal Democratic Party, however, certainly don't hide the fact that they are in favour of Britain as a multiculturalist nation. In the 1997 Labour Party General Election Manifesto, they explicitly said that "Britain is a multiracial and multicultural country." When Tony Blair, leader of the Labour Party at the time, won a landslide victory in the 1997 General Election, the effort to transform Britain into a culturally neutral space was kicked into full gear. Today, 54% of Conservative Party voters are in favour of multiculturalism,[7] and whilst Cameron once claimed state multiculturalism has failed, he has not explicitly suggested that it cannot work. Cameron

---

[7] Lord Ashcroft, "45 years on, do ethnic minorities remember 'rivers of blood'?" Lord Ashcroft Polls, 19th April 2013, http://lordashcroftpolls.com/2013/04/45-years-on-do-ethnic-minorities-remember-rivers-of-blood/

and his cabinet remained committed to multiculturalism throughout their years in government and were obsessed with forcing people into positions solely because of their race, religion or gender – as can be seen with his appointment of Sayeeda Warsi to his cabinet, who had failed to win a seat in the General Election. As a way of forcing her into a position of power (as she is both a woman and a Muslim), Cameron gave her a peerage. In 2014, Cameron's cabinet reshuffle resulted in the appointment of numerous little-known women, which has widely been criticised as nothing other than 'window dressing' by Unions, newspapers and the public at large.[8]

The Liberal Democrats, in coalition with the Conservative Party, are also major players in the establishment of multiculturalism as the 'standard' nature of Britain. With ethnic minority groups within the party, Diversity Engagement Groups, and a focus on "improving the diversity of our MPs in Parliament," [9] the party can be considered a major part of this Paradoxical Alliance.

Culturism

This chapter has outlined the basic actors in the Paradoxical Alliance, Islam and multiculturalism. It will also provide a method by which to untangle this noose knot and restore freedom of speech and sanity to the West: culturism. Culturism is the opposite of multiculturalism. People that believe in it are called 'culturists.' It is a powerful, rational solvent.

---

[8] "Cameron: New Cabinet team 'reflects modern Britain,'" ITV News, 16th July 2014, http://www.itv.com/news/update/2014-07-15/unions-attack-cabinet-reshuffle-as-window-dressing/
[9] Liberal Democrat official website, http://www.libdems.org.uk/diversity

A main goal of the culturist movement is reopening dialogue on issues that the multiculturalists have silenced. First of all, the very words 'culturism' and 'culturist' point to the fact that we are discussing cultural diversity, not race. As such, when the multiculturalists call you a racist for discussing the existence of cultural diversity, you can very correctly tell them that race and culture are different. Islam is not a race. Furthermore, you can assert your right to discuss cultural issues. They must accede. After all, their slogan "celebrate diversity" obliges them to engage in discussions concerning the reality of diversity. To survive, western nations must be able to discuss the very real importance of cultural diversity.

Culturism also has truth on its side because, in contradistinction to multiculturalism, it acknowledges that cultural diversity exists. Using the disarming words 'culturism' and 'culturist,' we should be able to discuss the reality of female genital mutilation without being called 'racist.'

Furthermore, multiculturalism is all-or-nothing. It allows absolutely no ascriptions of violence, female genital mutilation, or grooming to Muslims. Culturism is subtle. It does not say all Muslims practice female genital mutilation. It asks for a rational statistical study of cultural tendencies. If cultural diversity is real and important, we should like to be able to study cultural propensities.

Before leaving this chapter, I would like to introduce one more feature of culturism: it acknowledges that the West, in fact, does have a particular culture. The West stands for women's rights, the freedom of speech, the relative separation of church and state, individual conscience, the rights of homosexuals to live without harassment, democracy, non-violence and other liberal values. These are not universal values. Islam, for example, (not to mention China and numerous other non-Islamic countries) cherishes none of these values to the extent that the West does – if at all. They are not universal values. Diversity is real. Thus, culturism recognises that the Western sphere in general, and Britain in particular, have a culture and a need to protect it.

Multiculturalism denies that the West has a core traditional culture. It says that Britain is just as Muslim as it is Christian. On this basis, it supports Sharia courts on British soil. Culturism, on the other hand, recognises that Sharia courts are not British. They appear neither in our law nor our history, and fly in the face of the Rule of Law. And, as they are profoundly anti-western in attitude, they should not have any legal standing in western land. Britain should only recognize and promote British law and tradition. If you do not stand for something, you'll fall for anything. Culturism gives us something to stand for.

In the next chapter, we will look at how Islam affects British politics and how British, multiculturalist, and left-liberal politicians are pushing Islam whilst failing to recognize the threat to themselves and their ideologies which it poses. In short, I will be outlining how the Paradoxical Alliance is taking shape through political institutions.

CHAPTER TWO
Politics and Islam

Islam under the 2010-2015 Conservative and Liberal Democrat Coalition

Alliances and compromise are intrinsic to politics. This partially explains politicians' infamous inability to keep promises. It is as if every promise should have the following caveat: "If elected I promise to do so and so – provided I have enough votes to get it done." This also partially justifies the assertion that, 'It does not matter which party you vote for, they're all the same.'

These dynamics were illustrated in Britain's 2010 election: The Conservative Party didn't win enough Parliamentary seats to form a majority government, and so for the first time in thirty-six years a coalition government was formed. This meant that the Conservative Party's ability to enforce its own platform was diminished. The Conservatives had promised to repeal the Human Rights Act,[10] and David Cameron himself had offered a "cast iron guarantee" of a referendum on continued membership of the European Union.[11] Neither happened during his first term in government.

The need to form a coalition government can also be a convenient excuse for inaction if one is not committed to

---

[10] Travis, Alan, "Cameron pledges bill to restore British freedoms," The Guardian, 28th February 2009,
https://www.theguardian.com/politics/2009/feb/28/conservatives-human-rights

[11] Summers, Deborah, "David Cameron admits Lisbon treaty referendum campaign is over," The Guardian, 4th November 2009,
https://www.theguardian.com/politics/2009/nov/04/david-cameron-referendum-campaign-over

it. By taking strong actions, one risks alienating some voters and energizing one's opponent's base. A politician's safe course of action, electorally, is to do nothing and blame coalition dynamics. Of course, these dynamics irk voters. But when the constituent in question is an immigrant group, the dynamics discussed above can lead to culturist suicide; that is, a loss of sovereignty over the country's borders and a lack of ability to insist on the continuance of the traditional, majority culture. Herein this goes from being political dynamic to a matter of life and death.

When a constituency comprises a high proportion of immigrants, taking an anti-immigration position means electoral suicide. The 2010 election saw the number of Muslim Members of Parliament double from four to eight, with two being elected for the Conservative Party for the first time[12]. Over ninety Muslim candidates stood in the election and those that won relied heavily upon the substantial Muslim community and demographic within their constituencies which they represented. It goes without saying that the policies of those candidates would not have called for any restriction on immigration if they wished to secure their seat.

The Power of the Muslim Vote

A striking example of the power of the Paradoxical Alliance can be seen in the way that Muslims and multiculturalists vote. Labour's Shabana Mahmood, who won the Birmingham Ladywood seat in 2010 (taking the seat from Labour's Clare Short), shows the incredible power of the Muslim vote, supported by multiculturalist voters.

---

[12] Hasan, Mehdi, "Rejoice! The number of Muslim MPs has doubled," New Statesman, 7th May 2010, http://www.newstatesman.com/blogs/mehdi-hasan/2010/05/muslim-majority-labour-england

Mahmood actually increased the majority for Labour in this part of the country by 3,304 votes, despite the Labour Party having been in power for thirteen years and suffering low ratings in the opinion polls. In the 2015 election, she increased that majority again by 11,763 compared to her 2010 results, and by 15,067 compared to Clare Short's result in 2005. This is arguably a result of her appeal to the Islamic community in Birmingham Ladywood, as well as progressive and ethnic minority voters. This effect grants a great deal of power to progressives and those whose agenda is focused around transforming inner cities, and ultimately the whole nation, from a collectively culturist society to a multiculturalist society.

According to the 2011 census, the Ladywood region (not the whole parliamentary constituency) had 3,504 Muslims, making 11.6% of the population Muslim. This figure, of course, is not including those who did not fill in the form correctly or honestly, which is not uncommon in highly Islamic areas. Thirty-nine percent of the overall population were also born outside of England,[13] and there are more than forty mosques, community centres and large public prayer rooms available throughout Ladywood. These statistics don't even take into account the significant number of foreign nationals, foreign born and, specifically, Muslims throughout the rest of the Parliamentary constituency, which also includes Aston, Soho and Nechells, bringing the overall population to 126,693.

The first Muslim elected for the Conservative Party was Sajid Javid, who managed to hold the Bromsgrove seat and increase the majority by 11,000 – an even more

---

[13] QPZM Local Stats UK, http://ladywood.localstats.co.uk/census-demographics/england/west-midlands/birmingham/ladywood

impressive feat than that achieved by Mahmood. Rehman Christi also managed to create a substantial 8,500 vote majority in the newly-formed constituency of Gillingham and Rainham.

In Bethnal Green and Bow, Muslim Rushanara Ali also won a majority of 11,000 and Ajmal Masroor for the Liberal Democrats came second. In third place was the Respect Party's Abjol Miah.

With constituencies like these dotted throughout the UK, at first glance it's easy to see why the careerists in the major parties so often appease Islam. Though, put into a national perspective, it doesn't make much sense at all. There were only eight Muslim Members of Parliament elected in 2010, yet the political elite seem to be bending over backwards in a fight to become the most 'Muslim friendly' party. A notable example of the constant battle to be more diverse than the other parties is the promotion of Sayeeda Warsi to the House of Lords by Prime Minister David Cameron when she failed to win a seat in the General Election. Baroness Warsi became a Minister without Portfolio and sat as the co-Chairman of the party.

The move was controversial, given Warsi's relative inexperience, having only served as the Shadow Minister for Community Cohesion and Social Action since 2007. That position was created for her and was later abolished. Before that, she had no real political role and was considered a newcomer. The promotion to Minister without Portfolio and later to Chairman of the Conservative Party, all within the space of three years, is striking. Warsi later resigned from the Government on the 5th August 2014, claiming that she was unable to support Government policy relating to the conflict between Gaza and Israel. She also explained that she believes the exports of arms to Israel "must stop." It was clearer than ever on this day that Warsi's allegiance was to Islam, not the British people.

The Conservative-Islam Paradoxical Alliance

Owing to coalitional politics, national sovereignty is also compromised by immigrants winning regional elections. A conservative party without a strong electoral majority will need these constituencies to form a government. Therefore, even the national government's will to act – no matter how sincere - is compromised by these regional election results. So, having immigrant communities dotted across a nation can threaten its will to maintain its sovereignty. Once that happens the immigrant population will only grow. And, with their birth rates being higher than the national average, it means Britain can no longer hope to be a united, cohesive nation.

Herein we see a Paradoxical Alliance that many overlook, that between conservatives and Muslims. To see why this is a paradox, we need look no further than the word 'conservative.' To conserve means to keep. And, in the tradition of Britain's pre-eminent political writer, Edmund Burke, this means conserving Britain's culture. Just as much as anyone else in power, conservatives are multicultural. They regularly feature a diverse group of people in their literature. They perform 'outreach' to Muslims based on permitting them to retain their own distinct culture within Britain's borders. This is not conservative though.

A truly conservative government would be culturist - It would acknowledge that Britain has an ancient, traditional, majority culture. Britain's culture is distinct. It certainly does not include Islamic values such as Sharia. It does not include allowing opposing values to be promoted by public agencies. To conserve Britain's culture, conservatives need be culturist; they must insist on linguistic and cultural assimilation. Shy of this, if they are multicultural, they cannot be truly 'conservative' in any allowable meaning of the word.

So far, we have discussed how immigration can generically undermine national sovereignty. We could also include a large section on how, if possible, culturist dynamics could forestall such national disintegration. Such a discussion would involve policies such as loyalty oaths to Britain's version of church and state, as well as educational policies. Even with a hostile and oppositional culture such as Islam, extremism could be persecuted and assimilation promoted to the point where, along with border enforcement, a small moderate Muslim population might not destabilize Britain's cultural hegemony over its land.

Islam is a very hostile and foreign culture. Its values are completely incompatible with British values. But this problem is exacerbated because even conservatives have adopted multiculturalism. That means that they cannot and will not condemn Islam. They cannot and will not admit that cultural diversity includes values that are incompatible with any other value systems. It commits them to such a completely Pollyanna position, that they cannot bring themselves to admit to the existence of evil in the world.

The failure to acknowledge evil is the most dangerous part of multiculturalism. It says, at heart, that lions and zebras all hold compatible values. Zebras need not fear lions. It is kumbaya on steroids! So, Britain's politicians cannot begin to a) accept the idea that Islamic powers are using demographics to attack western civilization, and b) that we need to have a culturist mentality whereby we put our own cultural survival first and foremost as a governing priority. Under multiculturalism, all 'conservatives' can do is praise the 'vibrancy' that Islamic communities bring to Britain.

The 2015 General Election's 'Muslim Manifesto'

In April 2015, a month before the General Election, an Islamist group that called itself 'Muslim Engagement and Development' (MEND) claimed it could control the outcome of up to thirty seats and could thus be kingmakers for any coalitional government by offering significant amounts of money to Tory and Labour candidates who signed up to what they called their 'Muslim Manifesto,' a document released by the organisation which sets out goals it wants Members of Parliament to support or achieve.

The manifesto begins by proudly displaying that the UK population is now 4.8% Muslim, and 48% of those Muslims are aged twenty-four and under. Thus, the demographic threat inches ever closer. One might reasonably expect this (or any) immigrant group to explain its importance (power) to politicians. The manifesto does no such thing however – in fact it goes one step further. It commits politicians to an aggressive multiculturalism policy that actually outlaws all culturist sentiment in Britain. It requires that signatories:

1. Commit to (a) recording of Islamophobia as a category of hate crime by all police forces in England and Wales, as is currently done with other types of hate crime (b) working with social media companies to protect free speech while developing good guidelines to tackle hate speech online (c) consider primary legislation to deal with social media offences and hate speech online

2. Commit to media reform and the full implementation of the Royal Charter on a Leveson compliant regulator; support industry initiatives to promote positive, diverse representations of Muslims and minorities in the mainstream media.

3. Commit to offering Sharia compliant student loans to make higher and further education accessible to British Muslims; support the growth of the Sharia compliant financial services industry

4. Commit to fostering social cohesion and community resilience to all forms of extremism; support de-radicalisation programmes that work with Muslim communities not against them.

5. Commit to support for an independent Palestine and end of Israeli occupation by December 2017.

Here we see again why multiculturalism is so dangerous. It is not just a cute philosophy that liberals put on their bumper stickers and t-shirts, it is a criminal code. Not coincidentally, MEND's first policy outlaws criticizing Islam. In doing so, it calls noticing cultural diversity, 'Islamophobia.' This is ridiculous because it assumes that no culture could actually be aggressive. The notion that diversity could be so broad that it includes violent, angry, aggressive, theocratic values is, under this paradigm, irrational. Multiculturalists insist that this depth of diversity could not possibly exist and, as such, they wish to criminalize all such discussions as 'hate crime.'

From a culturist point of view, cultural diversity is very real. It includes evil cultural tendencies such as those noted above. It also assumes that Britain has a distinct unique traditional culture - and by definition, since the trait is not universal and diversity exists, Britain and western cultures need protection. Under MEND's multicultural program we not only have to deny that the West has a unique, non-universal culture, but saying that it does not include Islamic values becomes punishable by law. The pervasiveness of such threats, and the multicultural paradigm, means that 'conservatives' fear advocating a culturist position.

MEND is not just a fantasy group. It began winning support of politicians, including Kate Green who was the Shadow Equalities Minister for the Labour Party at the time. Green spoke at a March 2015 MEND event where she shared a platform with Abu Eesa Niamatullah, a Pakistani Imam and lecturer who has previously called the British population "animals" and demanded that "the Creator" (Allah) should "decide what the laws should be." Also on stage with Green and Niamatullah was the Conservative Party's Baroness Warsi.

In a leaked recording, the Daily Telegraph claimed that MEND's CEO, Sufyan Ismail, spoke about his organisation's ongoing negotiations with the Conservative and Labour leaderships.[14] The very fact that they were in negotiations with Labour is paradoxical. The second platform, which only allows positive depictions of Muslims, is pure multicultural, and since they are the multicultural party, this makes sense. The real paradoxical nature comes into play when multiculturalists advocate platform three. That is because supporting Sharia means enslaving two of their main constituents, women and gays. But, as we have

---

[14] Gilligan, Andrew, "Muslim group with links to extremists boasts of influencing election," The Telegraph, 4th April 2015, http://www.telegraph.co.uk/news/general-election-2015/11515630/Muslim-group-with-links-to-extremists-boasts-of-influencing-election.html

discussed, so-called 'conservatives' agreeing to support a foreign legal system in Britain is even worse.

The greatest paradox, the one between multiculturalist and culturist perspectives, appears in points number four and five. Four states that it wants the government to constructively work to end radicalization within the Muslim community (this will, of course, mean a huge infusion of taxpayer monies). And, number five states that the government must support Islamic expansion hostile to an outpost of western civilization, Israel. This shows that the multiculturalist pretences are only a smoke screen; they will not give up imposing Sharia in Britain or aggressive Islamic expansion globally.

Mass Muslim Electoral Fraud

In 2005 Britain was dubbed a 'banana republic' by Richard Mawrey QC,[15] a senior judge, who explained that there was "no realistic system in place to detect or prevent postal voting fraud at the general election." Mawrey found that thousands of postal votes had been stolen and changed by (or even completed by) Labour activists. He also noted that these actions were not uncommon or the actions of merely a few, but were widespread and performed with the full knowledge of the local Labour party branch. In Birmingham in particular, Mawrey found six Labour councillors had been carrying out the operation, where postal vote applications rose from 28,000 to 70,000.

A study for the Electoral Commission released in January 2015 by the University of Manchester and

---

[15] Mawrey Q.C., Richard, Election Petition Judgement: Birmingham 2004 Bordesley Green & Aston Wards (Labour fraud), http://law.slough.info/law44/law44p072.php

University of Liverpool,[16] warned of 'ethnic kinship voting' and suggested that Pakistani and Bangladeshi-origin communities (Muslim communities) share a wide range of "vulnerabilities" – including being "susceptible to becoming victims of electoral fraud." This is of course typical university/academic speak for "Muslim communities are the most likely to produce electoral fraud." Specifically, the report identified the main sources of this 'vulnerability' as:

- Language and knowledge barriers
- Community loyalties and pressures
- Kinship networks
- Lack of mainstream political party engagement
- Discrimination in candidate selection
- Insufficiency of safeguards for voting procedures
- Local economic deprivation

There is clearly a problem with electoral fraud in Muslim communities across the UK, and not only are local Labour party branches appeasing and allowing it, it would seem our academics and universities are making excuses for it too.

In 2005, it was beginning to become evident that Muslims were engaging in widespread electoral fraud, with Mawrey noting that the activity had been focused in areas with a large Muslim population – and ever since, the problem has escalated.

---

[16] University of Manchester, University of Liverpool, "Understanding electoral fraud vulnerability in Pakistani and Bangladeshi origin communities in England," Prepared for the Electoral Commission, Centre on Dynamics of Ethnicity, January 2015, http://www.electoralcommission.org.uk/__data/assets/pdf_file/0006/18 1257/Understanding-Electoral-Fraud-Jan-2015.pdf

Electoral fraud is not, however, an example of the Paradoxical Alliance. The reasons behind Muslim electoral fraud are open to debate. The fundamental question here though is, why is the Left supporting and defending Muslims who commit these crimes? How can the Labour Party and so-called 'anti-fascist' groups claim to wish to uphold democracy but at the same time defend people who are, a) religiously obliged to accept only the laws of Allah and, b) actively resisting the democratic system by making it work in their favour?

Islam in the Labour Party

The Labour Party has long been seen as the party for immigrants and for those in favour of continued mass immigration, and of course this has resulted in the party becoming the traditional party for Muslims. As the Muslim population in the UK has increased, the Labour Party's pandering to Islam has grown. In the 1997 election, where Tony Blair won in a landslide, Muslims voted in abundance for the Labour Party. In this election, 84% of the Bangladeshi community voted for Blair's New Labour, and 80% of the Pakistani community did the same, according to analyst Shamit Saggar.[17]

Today, the Labour Party has more Muslim MPs than any other party in the country, with nine being elected in the 2015 General Election. A number of these MPs had kept their seat from the previous election, namely Khalid Mahmood, Shabana Mahmood, Rushanara Ali, Yasmin Qureshi and Sadiq Khan. The presence of Muslim MPs is of course not the primary issue here, however. Sure, there is a question to be asked about the trustworthiness of Muslim

---

[17] Maguire, Kevin, "Wake-up call for party that took votes for granted," The Guardian, 19th June 2002,
https://www.theguardian.com/uk/2002/jun/19/september11.religion

MPs who are instructed by their holy book to deceive the kafir, but the primary issues are the agenda of the white British appeasers of Islam in the Labour Party, and the impact that Islam has on a party which could one day form another government.

Brown's Labour Party

Gordon Brown, the Labour Party Prime Minister from 2007 to 2010, regularly and publicly exclaimed that terrorism is not an Islamic issue – something that almost every elected politician in the UK and even America now parrots. His appeasement of Islam goes much further than this though. In 2007, newly-appointed Prime Minister Brown began manipulating language to push his politically correct, multiculturalist agenda. It was reported that Brown announced to his cabinet and staff that the word 'Muslim' should not be used when describing terrorist attacks and terrorists.[18] By banning the use of the term 'Muslim,' Brown was attempting to disassociate the Islamic religion with the barbaric acts of terrorists all over the world – and it stuck.

Notice how so many in the Western media now refer to Islamic State as the 'so-called Islamic State,' as if Muslims carrying out these atrocities across Syria and beyond aren't Islamic or Muslim. Naturally, Brown's staff called this a step towards striking "a consensual tone in relation to all communities across the UK,"[19] when in fact

[18] Hussain, Rashad, "Reformulating the Battle of Ideas: Understanding the Role of Islam in Counterterrorism Policy," Saban Centre at Brookings, August 2008, Analysis Paper 13, P. 6, http://www.brookings.edu/~/media/research/files/papers/2008/8/counterterrorism-hussain/08_counterterrorism_hussain.pdf
[19] Hall, Macer, "Brown: Don't say terrorists are Muslims," The Express, 3rd July 2007, http://www.express.co.uk/news/uk/12172/Brown-Don-t-say-terrorists-are-Muslims

this measure only affected the Muslim community and made it significantly easier for creeping Sharia to keep on creepin', and Muslim hate preachers to keep on preachin', without the 'good' name of Islam being tarnished. I'm not necessarily suggesting that Brown's agenda was to make the cause of Jihad easier, but I absolutely am suggesting that his part in this bizarre Paradoxical Alliance is significant and important. Brown is amongst the first Western leaders who have perpetuated the idea that Islam is peaceful in the name of "community cohesion."

I wonder how Gordon Brown would react to being forced to convert at the threat of beheading, how he'd feel seeing his daughter Jennifer being gang raped and then killed under the cries of "Alahu Akbar," and if he'd then still continue his mantra "this is the work of terrorists, not Muslims." Is Brown unaware that Muhammad himself was a violent man? Is he unaware that he had nine swords, his favourite of which he called the Dhu al-Faqar, the "Cleaver of Vertebrae"? If Islamic terrorists are not Muslims, does Brown believe that their "prophet" Muhammad was also not a Muslim?

Brown's dhimmitude, and the ignorance and appeasement of the Labour Party as a whole, is a prime example of the Paradoxical Alliance in the West. These left-multiculturalists, progressives and socialists bend over backwards to protect an ideology that would have them killed, enslaved or paying Jizya should they live in a real Islamic State.

Miliband's Labour Party

The next Labour leader after Brown was Ed Miliband, the younger brother of David Miliband who was the Labour Secretary of State for Foreign and

Commonwealth Affairs between 2007 and 2010. Ed Miliband was elected on the Union votes and despite being considered too 'mild' a candidate, he took on the role and fought the 2015 general election – and failed...miserably. Despite polls suggesting the Tories and Labour would be almost tied in quantity of Parliamentary seats won, Labour lost all but one of its Scottish seats to the Scottish National Party and gave the Conservative Party the most surprising majority in decades. Miliband's failure was certainly not a result of his inability to pander to the Muslim vote however. In fact, Miliband mastered the art of pandering to Islam and introduced the wildest proposal yet – a new blasphemy law that would make 'Islamophobia' illegal.[20]

Ed Miliband told the country that under a Miliband government, Islamophobia would be made an aggravated crime. Specifically, Miliband said:

> We are going to make it an aggravated crime. We are going to make sure it is marked on people's records with the police to make sure they root out Islamophobia as a hate crime.
>
> We are going to change the law on this so we make it absolutely clear of [sic] our abhorrence of hate crime and Islamophobia. It will be the first time that the police will record Islamophobic attacks right across the country.

During an interview with The Muslim News, Miliband then explained that the Muslim community is an "incredibly important, incredibly rich, incredible asset to our country." The claim is questionable, but at least Miliband didn't lie

---

[20] Kern, Soeren, "Britain's Labour Party Vows to Ban Islamophobia," The Gatestone Institute International Policy Council,30th April 2015, https://www.gatestoneinstitute.org/5665/uk-islamophobia-ban

about his intentions. Much like his predecessor Brown, Miliband was and still is committed to pandering to 4.5% of the population. His reason? The most obvious is that winning over Muslims can help you win seats – as was seen when MEND offered to be kingmakers of up to 30 seats. But in the grand scheme of things this is just a drop in the ocean. With 48% of Muslims in the UK being under 24, the number of Muslims eligible to vote is closer to three million.[21] This is merely 6-7% of the forty-five million-strong electorate of the UK. Miliband's commitment to such a small number of people when the traditional Labour voters, the white working class, still make up a significantly higher proportion of the electorate, raises plenty of questions.

Harriet Harman in the Labour Party

Miliband's colleague Harriet Harman is a major player in the Paradoxical Alliance too. Previously the Shadow Deputy Prime Minister and Shadow Secretary of State for Culture, Media and Sport, Harman praised segregation at Labour Party rallies during the 2015 General Election. On the 2nd May 2015, the Labour Party held a 'rally' in Birmingham, designed to engage with local voters. In attendance was Labour's Shabana Mahmood MP, along with a host of other MPs and local councillors. Pictures were revealed in the national press of the crowd which clearly showed men seated on one side of the room and women on the other. For a time, the Labour Party remained quiet on the issue – but then piped up Harriet Harman, Labour's go-to radical feminist. Harman defended the sexist segregation (which was of course done to keep local Muslim voters happy) as "better than a men-only meeting" and claimed that boycotting the event would have been rude. Sure.

---

[21] http://mend.org.uk/wp-content/uploads/2015/03/MEND-Muslim-Manifesto-GE2015_LowRes.pdf

From a woman who introduced the notorious Equality Act of 2010, a piece of legislation that made it legal to discriminate against white, straight males in the workforce, it is hard to believe that she would have backed down if a Christian Labour Party group (if any such thing really exists any more) had segregated their audience. The Paradoxical Alliance is shown here perfectly. Harman, despite her notorious passion for giving women special treatment, backed down like a neutered dog and let this anti-Western, unpleasant treatment go unquestioned. Why? Why would a feminist ally herself with such ideas and people, and why, pray tell, did Shabana Mahmood MP not say anything despite claiming to be passionate about "social justice, fairness and equality"?[22] Perhaps Harman's priorities lie with paedophiles, and in turn, proponents of a religion that idolises a paedophile as its prophet. Harman, along with her husband Jack Dromey MP (Labour) and Patricia Hewitt, formerly a Labour Cabinet Minister, worked for the National Council for Civil Liberties in the 1970s – a group which granted affiliate status to the Paedophile Information Exchange (PIE).[23] PIE lobbied for the legalisation of sex with children. Harman still refuses to apologise for her involvement. Nice woman.

Incidentally, Jack Dromey publicly commented on my election campaign in the Batley and Spen constituency in 2016 (where I campaigned for justice for the victims of

---

[22] Shabana Mahmood official website,
http://www.shabanamahmood.org/about-shabana
[23] Hope, Christopher, "Harriet Harman admits paedophile group joined her civil libterties group in the 1970s," The Telegraph, 24th February 2014,
http://www.telegraph.co.uk/news/politics/labour/10659169/Harriet-Harman-admits-paedophile-group-joined-her-civil-liberties-group-in-the-1970s.html

Muslim rape gangs). The Labour MP called my candidacy "obscene, outrageous and contemptible."[24]

Jeremy Corbyn's Labour Party

In September 2015, veteran socialist Jeremy Corbyn was elected as the new leader of the Labour Party with 59% of the vote. Corbyn has the support of the unions – traditionally a huge part of the Labour support and a huge influence on the result of their leadership elections – but he has also won support outside the unions. In fact, Corbyn relied on new Labour Party members, as well as young Social Justice Warriors, to achieve his landslide victory.

Throughout conservative, culturist, and traditionalist circles, Corbyn has been a bit of a laughing stock. "He will confine the Labour Party to electoral history!" conservatives have shouted with glee – and the fact that many frontbench Labour MPs have since resigned the shadow cabinet and returned to the backbench, suggests many in his party agree. But I don't think this is really the case. Whether he's ousted as party leader, or remains until the 2022 General Election, Corbyn is in a prime position to change the nature of British politics. He is a communist – let's just get this out of the way. It's not even like he's ashamed of it, either – he's sung Bandiera Rossa at Labour rallies throughout 2015, and at innumerable other events throughout his political life. If you're not familiar with Bandiera Rossa, it is one of the most prominent songs from the Italian labour movement. It goes:

Forward people, to the rescue
Red Flag, Red Flag

---

[24] Sorrentino, Alessandro, "Jack Dromey MP blasts decision to contest murdered Jo Cox's seats as 'obscene'," Birmingham Mail, 20th June 2016, http://www.birminghammail.co.uk/incoming/jack-dromey-mp-blasts-decision-11498338

Forward people, to the rescue
Red Flag will triumph.

Red Flag will be triumphant,
Red Flag will be triumphant,
Red Flag will be triumphant,
Long live communism and freedom.

As the leader of the official opposition, Corbyn has presented a communist/socialist agenda through the mainstream media and institutions. He has helped shift political discussion and given a voice to young university students who are interested only in destroying gender roles and pretending that women are men. Socialism is no longer confined to the backbench nor to the smaller pressure groups and Labour Party-funded "anti-fascist" thug groups. It is mainstream again and will need to be countered with equally radical conservatism. But this is beside the point. Since his election, Corbyn and his communist colleagues have worked for Islam and promoted (or at least, wilfully ignored) Jihad – making them yet another example of the Paradoxical Alliance between politicians and Islam in modern Britain. Corbyn's dream of 'equality' flies in the face of the agenda of Muslim politicians and activists, and yet, he considers Hamas and Hezbollah his friends.[25]

In 2003, Corbyn was a delegate of the Cairo 'Stop the War' conference where officials advocated for a military struggle against Western coalition forces.[26] Corbyn was also

---

[25] "Corbyn Invited Terrorists and War Criminals into Parliament," Order-Order Guido Fawkes, 15th June 2015, http://order-order.com/2015/06/15/corbyn-invited-terrorists-and-war-criminals-into-parliament/

[26] Swinford, Steven, "Jeremy Corbyn attended Iraq conference that called for military struggle against Coalition," The Telegraph, 7th September 2015,

the national chair of the Stop the War Coalition until a week after his election as Labour leader. He has still not denounced the group's advocacy of military struggle against coalition forces in Iraq and its open endorsements of attacks against Western soldiers in the name of Islamic forces across the East.

Corbyn's campaign team during the Labour leadership election released a statement claiming that he is "proud to speak at every opportunity of understanding between Christian, Hindu, Jewish, Muslim and other faiths."[27] This is hard to believe considering Corbyn has not spoken at any major Christian events (they probably wouldn't have him anyway), together also with the fact that he has given speeches at Al Quds Day events in London where anti-Semitic posters were proudly displayed by Muslim attendees and pro-Palestine activists.

Corbyn, as well as fellow MP Gerald Kaufman, was seen at the April 2013 Deir Yassin Remembered Commemoration – an event and organisation run by Paul Eisen, a self-professed Holocaust denier. Eisen wrote a blog post that has since been removed (but was reported on by The Daily Mail,[28] The Express, and a host of other newspapers, where he allegedly talked about his 15-year

---

http://www.telegraph.co.uk/news/politics/labour/11849934/Jeremy-Corbyn-attended-Iraq-conference-that-called-for-military-struggle-against-Coalition.html

[27] Mason, Rowena, "Jewish Labour MP hits out at Jeremy Corbyn's record on antisemitism," The Guardian, 14th August 2015, http://www.theguardian.com/politics/2015/aug/14/jewish-labour-mp-jeremy-corbyn-antisemitism-record-ivan-lewis

[28] Wallis Simons, Jake, "EXCLUSIVE: Jeremy Corbyn's 'long-standing links' with notorious Holocaust denier and his 'anti-Semitic' organisation revealed," The Daily Mail, 7th August 2015, http://www.dailymail.co.uk/news/article-3187428/Jeremy-Corbyn-s-links-notorious-Holocaust-denier-revealed.html

contact with Corbyn. According to the blog post, Eisen allegedly explained that he had barely begun his pitch to Corbyn before he had lifted out his cheque book and was offering the holocaust denier money.

Corbyn claims that Eisen was not a Holocaust denier at this stage, and that any donation would only have been made in a collection bucket at an event held many years ago. This is of course a lie as there is photographic evidence, courtesy of DYR itself, of Corbyn attending their 2013 event.

Jeremy Corbyn's Labour leadership campaign website claimed that his policies are based on "justice, freedom, solidarity and equality for all" – but his endorsement of a Holocaust denier, "friendship" with Hezbollah and Hamas, support for extremist pro-Palestinian groups and claim that the murder of Osama Bin Laden was a "tragedy," all suggest that he is a very angry man indeed. How can this man claim to believe in justice and equality for all when at the same time, he is endorsing attacks against our own military and associating with groups that want to see the destruction of Israel and murder of Jews?

It's quite possible that Corbyn is actually entirely innocent. Perhaps his egalitarianism, socialism and obsession with state control in the name of 'equality' blinds him to the fact that he is supporting an ideology that wants to see the destruction of the West and murder of people like him. This is the best-case scenario and it makes him one of the best examples of the Paradoxical Alliance plaguing the West. At worst, Corbyn is a collaborator who is a part of the jihad cause. Given Corbyn's decades of experience working for the hard left, I suspect the former. Nonetheless he's a happy idiot.

Sadiq Khan as London Mayor

On May 7th 2016 the Labour Party won the London Mayoral elections, replacing famous Tory mayor Boris Johnson with a Muslim candidate by the name of Sadiq Khan. A former Shadow Secretary of State for Justice, and former Lord Chancellor, Khan is a prominent figure in the Labour Party. He achieved more votes in the London Mayoral Election than any other candidate in history, achieving 1,310,143 votes and beating the Tory candidate by 315,529.

Despite being a stalwart of Britain's premier social justice and equality party however, Khan has terrifying links. At the time of his election, the new London Mayor had already shared a platform with five known Islamic extremists at political meetings where women were made to use separate entrances and sit apart from the men in the audience. One such event, advertised as the "Friends of Al-Aqsa in conjunction with Tooting Islamic Centre Present: PALESTINE – THE SUFFERING STILL GOES ON," saw both Sadiq Khan and Jeremy Corbyn billed to attend. It took place on Sunday 19th September 2004, but Corbyn claims he didn't eventually attend. Guests and speakers included Ibrahim Hewitt, who had previously written booklets that labelled homosexuality a "great sin", and which explain how stoning to death is the appropriate punishment for adulterers.[29]

Daud Abdullah, a Muslim who organised a boycott of Holocaust Memorial Day in 2005, was also in attendance. At this time, Abdullah was the Deputy Secretary General of the Muslim Council of Britain.

---

[29] Hewitt, Ibrahim, "What Does Islam Say?" The Muslim Educational Trust, April 2004, https://www.hurryupharry.org/wp-content/uploads/2009/03/ibrahim-hewitt.pdf

His snubbing of the Holocaust Memorial Day is by no means his only crime, either. In fact, in 2009 Abdullah signed the Istanbul Declaration which called for violence against British armed forces and attacks against Israel.[30]

Khan's own actions (not just those of the people he shared platforms with) speak volumes though. After being elected Mayor of London, Khan set out to enforce Sharia throughout the capital city, starting with his push for an "online hate crime hub" that was designed to silence critics of Islam. In August 2016, it was reported that Khan's office had secured millions of pounds in funding for the "Online hate crime hub", which has been set up in partnership with all of the major social media networks. The move was welcomed by the Metropolitan Police[31] (the police force for London and Greater London) with a spokesman explaining:

> The Metropolitan Police Service is committed to working with our partners, including the mayor, to tackle all types of hate crime including offences committed online.

Internet users who became victims of the new measures would be prosecuted under Section 127 of the Communications Act 2003 which criminalises the use of a "public electronic communications network in order to cause

---

[30] Vardi, Daphna, "British Muslim leader signs Istanbul declaration," Jewish Telegraphic Agency, 8th March 2009, http://www.jta.org/2009/03/08/news-opinion/world/british-muslim-leader-signs-istanbul-declaration

[31] Deacon, Liam, "London Mayor to Set Up Police 'Online Hate Crime Hub' in 'Partnership' with Social Media Firms," Breitbart, 16th August 2016, http://www.breitbart.com/london/2016/08/16/london-mayor-to-set-up-police-online-hate-crime-hub-in-partnership-with-social-media-firms/

annoyance, inconvenience, or needless anxiety."[32]   Those who are found to be "hateful" online can face up to six months in prison or a fine of up to £5,000. This is literally the enforcement of Sharia, which explicitly bans the criticism of Islam and its prophet.

Indeed, the penalty for those who cause mischief against Allah and His Messenger (Muhammad) and contrive corruption upon the earth is that they be killed or crucified or that their hands and feet be cut off from opposite sides or that they be exiled from the land (Qur'an 5:33).

Khan provided legal defence for Zacarias Moussaoui, a terrorist involved with 9/11, and who confessed to being an Al Qaeda member. He also provided support for his childhood friend, Babar Ahmad, a man who was said to have been responsible for "inspiring a generation of extremists." Khan drove over 100 miles to meet with Ahmad, where his conversation was secretly recorded by police.[33] Ahmad was held under suspicion of running a website that supported Osama Bin Laden and which raised funds to assist the Taliban.

He also provided legal representation for the Nation of Islam when the group successfully took its case to the High Court, overturning a ban on its leader Louis Farrakhan

---

[32] Communications Act 2003, c.21, Part 2, Chapter 1, Offences relating to networks and services, Section 127, http://www.legislation.gov.uk/ukpga/2003/21/section/127

[33] Devlin, Amanda, "London Mayor Sadiq Khan was bugged by a police officer when he visited terror suspect in prison," The Sun, 12th May 2016, https://www.thesun.co.uk/archives/news/1172635/london-mayor-sadiq-khan-was-bugged-by-a-police-officer-when-he-visited-terror-suspect-in-prison/

from entering the United Kingdom.[34] The ban had been in place for 15 years owing to Farrakhan's remarks about Jews.

Khan is no friend to the progressive left, and yet his victory in London is still considered a great win for the anti-racism, anti-bigotry, and anti-xenophobia cause. Is it any surprise that his win was so gigantic though when, according to the 2011 census,[35] some 36.7% of London's population is foreign born, with 3,082,000 residents born outside of the UK in updated 2014 statistics.[36]

The Islamic Forum of Europe

The involvement with, and appeasement of Islam by the Labour Party stretches beyond the public sphere and into the shady depths of back room deals too. It was reported in 2010 by Andrew Gilligan of the Daily Telegraph, that the Islamic Forum of Europe had been infiltrating the Labour Party. According to a report on 27th February 2010, Gilligan reported that the then-Environment Minister, Jim Fitzpatrick, had claimed that the IFE had created a secret party within Labour, as well as a number of other political parties. Fitzpatrick explained that the IFE, an organisation which openly promotes the creation of an Islamic State in Britain and Europe, was:

---

[34] Dyer, Clare, "High court overturns 15-year ban on Farrakhan," The Guardian, 1st August 2001,
https://www.theguardian.com/uk/2001/aug/01/race.world3
[35] Office of National Statistics, 2011 Census, Key Statistics for Local Authorities in England And Wales,
http://www.ons.gov.uk/ons/rel/census/2011-census/key-statistics-for-local-authorities-in-england-and-wales/rft-table-qs203ew.xls
[36] Office of National Statistics, Migration, Population by Country of Birth and Nationality,
http://www.ons.gov.uk/ons/rel/migration1/population-by-country-of-birth-and-nationality/2014/rft-table-5-pop-by-cob-jan-14-to-dec-14.xls

...acting almost as an entryist organisation, placing people within the political parties, recruiting members to those political parties, trying to get individuals selected and elected so they can exercise political influence and power, whether it's at local government level or national level. They are completely at odds with Labour's programme with our support for secularism.

Is the IFE really actually at odds with the values of the Labour Party, though? As one of the primary players in the Paradoxical Alliance in the UK, the Labour Party is complicit in the implementation of Sharia throughout our society. Perhaps, in fact, it is Jim Fitzpatrick who is completely at odds with Labour's programme of bowing down to Sharia.

The infiltration of the Labour Party by the IFE came in the form of efforts to corrupt the party in East London. This is no conspiracy theory – IFE activists admitted to undercover reporters that they had 'a lot of influence and power' in Tower Hamlets, and boy did they ever! The activists had established their own group within the Labour Party and had been given access to more than £10 million in taxpayer's money – and the greatest irony is that this money came from government programmes that were setup to prevent 'violent extremism.'[37] Jim Fitzpatrick is commendable in his public 'outing' of the issue, but he was not joined by a great mass of Labour supporters. In fact, it seemed the IFE bloc within East London Labour had begun gaining traction and support from local members, this despite undercover reporters for Channel 4's 'Dispatches'

---

[37] Gilligan, Andrew, "Islamic radicals 'infiltrate' the Labour Party," The Telegraph, 27th February 2010, http://www.telegraph.co.uk/news/politics/labour/7333420/Islamic-radicals-infiltrate-the-Labour-Party.html

discovering their opposition to democracy, support for Sharia, and even mocking of black people.

The IFE began enforcing Sharia on people throughout East London and their local community, and of course within the Labour Party – which should come as no surprise if you are aware that the leaders of the group previously arranged meetings with allies of the Taliban, as well as men involved with the 9/11 attacks and 1993 World Trade Centre bombing. It really does beg the question – how were these people able to get away with so much, and why do these types gravitate so easily to the Labour Party? Could it possibly be that Labour leaders and members are so obsessed with being seen as progressive and accepting that they are perfectly willing to allow these types into their party on both a local and national level?

Lutfur Rahman's Historic Electoral Fraud

IFE members and supporters in East London Labour are also said to have assisted Lutfur Rahman become leader of Tower Hamlets Council. A number of councillors and former councillors have made claims that Rahman was supported by the IFE, and of course when he was put in charge of the local finances, funds began streaming from the local government and into IFE groups. Rahman also ended secular projects and began instructing schools to dismiss classes during Eid, even if the students were not Muslim.

Rahman was the leader of Tower Hamlets council for the Labour Party between 2008 and 2010, and soon went on to become the first directly-elected mayor of Tower Hamlets. This time, however, it was as an independent. Rahman enjoyed widespread support from the local Muslim community and was re-elected as mayor in 2014. It was on April 23rd, 2015, however, that the Election Court found him "personally guilty of corrupt or illegal practices," or both even, under the Representation of the People Act 1983. This became one of the most spectacular examples of election fraud in the UK. In fact, Rahman became the first person since the 19th Century to be found guilty in a court of law of unlawfully using religious influence in his election campaign.

The judge eventually found in 2015 that Rahman was guilty of running his campaign "on the basis that it was the religious duty of faithful Muslims to vote for him", and that up to 300 votes were made by individuals posing to be other voters. The Election Commissioner, in a rare act of sanity and clarity, said that the Lutfur Rahman case "starkly demonstrated what happens when those in authority are afraid to confront wrongdoing for fear of allegations of racism and Islamophobia" – and he was right. Questions surrounding Rahman's campaign were regularly knocked down, and even after the judge's ruling that there was wrongdoing, left-multiculturalists from the Socialist Worker's Party along with leading figures from trade unions and Labour, all rallied in support of Rahman claiming that he had been "forced out by racism." At an event on April 30th, 2015 Rahman attended a public meeting with:

- John Rees (People's Assembly)
- Christine Shawcroft (Labour Party NEC)
- Andrew Murray (Chief of Staff, Unite the Union)
- Lindsey German (Stop the War Coalition)
- Salma Yaqoob
- John McLoughlin (Branch Secretary of Tower Hamlets Unison)
- Weyman Bennett (Unite Against Fascism)

The event was entitled "Defend Democracy in Tower Hamlets!," and clearly showed how Rahman, despite having been found guilty for breaking election rules, had the liberal left wrapped around his little finger.

Annette Macki of 'Socialist Worker' also wrote a piece in which she explained:

> The judgement perpetuates the racist myth of Muslims as passive zombies manipulated by their leaders. It says, 'A distinction must be made between a sophisticated, highly educated and politically literate community and a community which is traditional, respectful of authority and, possibly, not fully integrated with the other communities living in the same area'. It upholds the claim that Rahman used 'spiritual influence.' Mawrey cites a letter signed by 101 imams stating it was a 'religious duty' to vote. But there was no outcry in March when a letter from Catholic bishops was read out at masses across England and Wales urging people to 'think carefully' about who to vote for in the general election. [38]

It is evident that Macki is either engaging in purposeful deception or is simply blind to the quite obvious fact that urging voters to perform their 'religious duty' is very different to telling voters to "think carefully."

With figures from trade unions, the Labour Party and pressure groups like Unite Against Fascism, Rahman was laughing all the way home with his support from Britain's leading progressive leftists, all of whom would in fact be

---

[38]https://tendancecoatesy.wordpress.com/2015/04/29/lutfur-rahman-forced-out-by-racism-says-socialist-worker-as-former-mayor-hand-picks-successor/

considered the enemy by Rahman's friends in the IFE. Perhaps these 'defenders of democracy' would benefit from reading even just a few of the 100+ verses of hate and violence in the Qur'an that call for the death or submission of the kafir.

Qur'an 8:12: "I will cast terror into the hearts of those who disbelieve. Therefore strike off their heads and strike off every fingertip of them."

Qur'an 9:5: "So when the sacred months have passed away, then slay the idolaters wherever you find them, and take them captive and besiege them and lie in wait for them in every ambush, then if they repent and keep up prayer and pay the poor-rate, leave their way free to them."

Qur'an 9:123: "O you who believe! fight those of the unbelievers who are near to you and let them find in you hardness."

UKIP's Pandering to Islam

The United Kingdom Independence Party (UKIP) was formed in 1993, and in 2014 the party managed to achieve 27.5% of the national vote in the European Union elections.[39] This pushed the Conservative Party to third place and lost the party seven seats in total.

UKIP, when led by its former chairman Lord Pearson, openly tackled Islam, and Pearson continues to talk

---

[39] "Maps of UKIP, Labour, Tory, Greens and Lib Dem Support," BBC News, 26th May 2014, http://www.bbc.co.uk/news/uk-politics-27576104

about the Islamic threat today.[40] In recent years, however, UKIP has stood extremist Muslims as candidates in elections and has removed members and candidates who suggest there might be an issue with Islam in Britain. In the 2014 local elections, UKIP stood Ummer Farooq, a 29-year-old Muslim, in Waltham Forest. Farooq attracted controversy when he claimed that Remembrance Day poppies represented "occultism" and that the 9/11 attacks were staged by the United States.[41] Numerous UKIP candidates and members have been removed from the party for questioning or attacking Islam too, including Eric Kitson who shared allegedly 'offensive' material and jokes about Muslims on his Facebook page.

Magnus Nielsen, formerly the Chairman of North London UKIP and the candidate for Hampstead and Kilburn in 2015, was also removed from UKIP. He claims that his expulsion came after he suggested that mosques and the Islamic clergy should be licensed in order to ensure that the doctrines taught were in accordance with the principles set out in the Universal Declaration of Human Rights. UKIP chairman Nigel Farage was contacted by Nielsen many times and gave no reply.

Farage has also rejected offers from the Dutch Party for Freedom to join a European alliance, owing to the anti-Islamic nature of the party.[42]

---

[40] "Ex-UKIP leader Lord Pearson warns of Islamist threat," BBC News, 20th November 2013, http://www.bbc.co.uk/news/uk-politics-25007869

[41] Glaze, Ben, "UKIP election hopeful in huge U-turn over Remembrance Sunday and 9/11 Twitter insults," The Mirror, 27th April 2014, http://www.mirror.co.uk/news/uk-news/ummer-farooq-ukip-election-hopeful-3464369

[42] Waterfield, Bruno, "Geert Wilders invites Nigel Farage to join anti-EU alliance," The Telegraph, 13th November 2013,

There has also been considerable flip flopping on the religious slaughter policy under Nigel Farage, and the party continues to reject membership from anybody who has previously been associated with known 'Islamophobic' groups, such as the English Defence League.

UKIP has made it clear that it is not a conservative culturist party. Farage may talk the talk about the failure of multiculturalism, but his party continues to support it and demonises culturist activists. This is a matter of life or death, and if Britain is to survive and become culturist, it is necessary for UKIP to be challenged by its members, supporters and by parties across Europe. This pandering has continued under Paul Nuttall, who despite introducing a burqa ban policy, deselected Anne Marie Waters as candidate for Lewisham East in the 2017 General Election because of her comments about Islam.

The pandering to Islam is also paradoxical for UKIP. The party's primary aim is to get Britain out of the European Union, which it sees as undemocratic (and this has, of course, happened after the Brexit vote of 2016). However, its support of Islam in Britain equates to a support of theocracy. Islam is incompatible with Western democracy as Muslims consider Allah as their ruler and take his laws from the clerics. The Qur'an also tells us that there should be no room for man-made law.

Qur'an 18:26: "Allah…makes none to share in His Decision and His Rule."

---

http://www.telegraph.co.uk/news/worldnews/europe/eu/10447939/Geert-Wilders-invites-Nigel-Farage-to-join-anti-EU-alliance.html

Qur'an 33:36: "It is not fitting for a Believer, man or woman, when a matter has been decided by Allah and His Messenger to have any option about their decision."

The Paradox

There are two primary examples of the Paradoxical Alliance in modern politics. The first is that politics is not democratic. Islam rejects democracy as mentioned in the last section. This suggests that many Muslims perhaps misunderstand their religion. It also suggests that many Muslims may very well know that their religion rejects man-made law and are using a system they oppose to benefit them – as we have seen in the widespread electoral fraud committed in Muslim communities.

The second is that politicians across all main parties are dedicated to the representation of Islam, despite the fact that Islam rejects the very multiculturalist, feminist and often progressive, socialist policies which they campaign for.

CHAPTER THREE
University and the National Union of Students

The University of Liverpool

In the autumn of 2011 I enrolled in the University of Liverpool's Political Science program with high hopes. On a campus which is surrounded by some stunning architecture, I expected to learn from and joust with great professors who had spent their entire lives considering philosophical roots and detailed implementation of political science concepts. Instead, within two years, the University had expelled me for questioning the government's dogma, multiculturalism.

Our whole nation needs to care about such expulsions. They reveal a Kafkaesque – Orwellian thought control system employed by universities, which those who go along with it do not see. When the universities create the illusion of free speech but remove those who disagree, it leads remaining students to believe that no diversity of opinion exists; the distance makes those expelled easier to demonise. The British government has taken on the same position towards its citizens that the University took to me.

This chapter will include a personal story. I will discuss my experiences at the University of Liverpool, where I was demonised and targeted by educators and students. I will also outline the nature of the Paradoxical Alliance in the National Union of Students and action taken by the government to intervene in an ongoing crisis within British universities.

The National Union of Students

The National Union of Students (NUS) is a confederation of student unions across the UK. Currently, there are more than six-hundred unions that make up the NUS, which accounts for more than 95% of the student unions that exist in the country. Founded in 1922, today it is the biggest player in dictating student politics.

The NUS decide on political associations for students and actively bans groups it believes to be bad for students. Like an overprotective mother, the NUS prevent students from learning from people they believe will potentially change the thought processes of their impressionable minds.

The NUS exert control over student affairs in almost all universities, but that's not to say the universities themselves are any better. In fact, in many cases the university staff can be much worse. Educational institutions across the UK widely adopt "equality and diversity" policies which stop people from openly expressing their opinions if they go beyond the Marxist rhetoric of most lecturers.

Make no mistake - British universities have been taken over. This is a growing issue in the United States, but in Britain there is not a single university left that encourages critical thinking. Students are no longer encouraged to expand their horizons and learn about opposing worldviews. Instead, the multicultural left, and feminists, are mollycoddled and protected from anything that is considered even remotely conservative or right of centre. The universities – and that includes the lecturers, university societies and students – also bow down to political correctness and Islam.

The best way to introduce these problems would be to detail my experiences at the University of Liverpool. I was removed from university for holding and espousing views that were not liked by staff, students, or local political groups

– and for sharing content on Twitter that was considered unacceptable. To be clear, the University suggested that the politics I engaged in, along with my online activity, were considered "misconduct."

My Expulsion

In 2012, I began an organisation called the National Culturists. My intention was to group like-minded conservative and culturist students within the university. I based my ideas on Dr John Press's book Culturism: A Word, A Value, Our Future.

Just weeks after starting the course, I was being harassed on campus. I was regularly stopped in the street and verbally abused. There were multiple attempts to physically attack me, and I even found posters on the wall of the library and hallways which compared me to the mass murderer Anders Breivik. It reached a point where the local police arranged to meet me to discuss my safety. And why? Well, I'd attempted to start a university society that celebrated British culture.

On one occasion, some friends and I distributed leaflets at the university which called on students to celebrate British and Western culture. We were met by a hoard of "anti-fascists" who stole leaflets from us, screamed in our faces, made threats to shoot me dead and followed us through the campus until we were forced to bundle into a cab and get away from those screaming lunatics. Of course, I was already aware of Liverpool's large 'anti-fascist' organisation, and so I understood the risks, which is why I had decided in advance to take a bodyguard with me. No student should need a body guard on campus.

In 2012, I wrote an article entitled "Modern Racism, Discrimination and Fascism in the University of Liverpool." The University demanded that I take down the article, presumably because they believed it portrayed the University in a bad light. I had written about examples of anti-Semitism I had found across campus, which included students walking around the University with images depicting bombs landing on the Star of David.[43] I was concerned that this had not been investigated by the school.

Being a person of morals, I decided to write an article about the situation. But rather than show appreciation for potentially helpful criticism, rather than applaud diversity of opinion on campus, the University disciplined me and gave me another warning on the basis that I was breaking school rules. I felt like Socrates. When asked what his punishment should be, said "Free dinners for the rest of my life." But, like Socrates, I could also smell the hemlock.

An extract from the article reads:

> If the National Union of Students is so pro-equality, and wants a quality learning experience for all, then why are the National Culturists attacked for being culturist, and why on earth do they not promote the possibility of a culturist education on top of multiculturalist education?

And this is a valid point; why is education only one-sided? Surely by teaching students that multiculturalism is the only "default" philosophy for Great Britain limits their understanding when they are not given the counter

---

[43] W, Joseph, "Liverpool Guild of Students President stands proudly by anti-Semitic poster," Hurry Up Harry, 22nd August 2011, http://hurryupharry.org/2011/08/22/liverpool-guild-of-students-president-stands-proudly-by-antisemitic-poster/

argument; that Britain's unique culture should be celebrated, and this is what every Western nation must strive to maintain? Surely any university which encourages critical thinking should at least permit some criticism of multiculturalism? Going one stage further, why not include classes that actually advocate the traditional alternative – a culturist education?

By demanding I take the article down, and not pursuing those responsible for cases of explicit race hatred and anti-Semitism, the school had demonstrated its unwillingness to change and its hatred for freedom of speech. It also showed clear political bias in favour of the race-and-culture-hating Left.

This, however, was only the beginning. I was also disciplined for making a clear point about the importance of freedom of speech, and how the Left puts emotion over fact.

In early 2013, I tweeted an image I came across online. The image was published by a rather unpleasant white supremacist group (who I in no way condone), but it contained a message that I knew would illustrate a point brilliantly – and that point is that the multicultural left, and the perpetual victims who study at university, consider certain facts to be offensive. Whether you're telling them that Muslims consider a paedophile to be their perfect man, or that statistically the Ashkenazi Jews have the highest IQs, they see nothing but offense and, what they call, bigotry and ignorance.

Of course, this couldn't be further from the truth. To be a bigot one must be intolerant of ideas one dislikes. To be ignorant, one must be lacking in knowledge or evidence. One is neither of these things if one takes evidence and comes to a conclusion based on said evidence. These two words, then, more accurately describes those very people who take offence.

This is the point I made when I tweeted this image. It suggested that if a person does not want to catch AIDS, then they should consider not having sex with intravenous drug abusers, bisexuals, and blacks. It also stated that black males are fourteen times as likely as white men to be HIV carriers. In actual fact, it is specifically black homosexual males that are fourteen times more likely to be HIV positive than white homosexual males, according to a study entitled "Back of the Line: The State of AIDS Among Black Gay Men in America."

The US Centers for Disease Control and Prevention reported that around 44% of all new HIV infections among adults and adolescents were African Americans – making black men seven times more likely than white men (regardless of their sexuality) to carry the disease.

So am I a bigot for tweeting this image? It wasn't even something I agreed with – I was just curious to see if my critics would respond to it on factual grounds, or simply opt-to call me a "bigot."[44] According to the students at my former university, I was. I continued with my provoking by suggesting that our campus could benefit from the image as posters.

Would it not be positive for universities to have material that promotes discussion about such a terrible affliction? Surely it would be more constructive for students to be aware of these facts, as opposed to burying their head in the sand and hoping that nothing offensive manages to slip

---

[44] And in all honestly, I was really just trying to be a bit of a dick to anyone who would be offended by the image.

through the grains and penetrate their poor, fearsome eardrums? Apparently not, because my University was once again soon on my case over the issue.

In a letter between two members of University staff, which was later provided to me at my request, I read how a reporter from The Huffington Post had contacted the University to ask about some of my tweets.

The letter reads:

> On 4th April 2013, the press office was contacted by The Huffington Post about tweets by Mr Buckby linking Islam to paedophilia. On 5th April, an article appeared online showing an offensive picture tweeted by Mr Buckby, which advised readers to avoid having sex with 'blacks' as they were more likely to have aids.

Well sorry, but it's true. Despite one's feelings about the subject, those are the facts; it's a correct statement after all. It wasn't so much the content which I was concerned with, rather making the point that a student ought to feel perfectly at ease in making a statement of fact without fear either of intimidation by one's peers, or being called "racist", and certainly not fearing any recrimination from the University for doing so. The previous letter went on to offer me a meeting and a "final warning."

Never once had I suggested that black people are inferior, that I hate them, or that these statistics mean that black people are worth less than white people. No, I had simply published tweets which showed how the multicultural left would rather cry 'racism' and be offended than actually discussing such issues and offering possible solutions.

However much people may wish to deny it, these statistics come from reputable sources; we cannot make appropriate policy, or suggest policies as political science students, if said policies are not based on facts. If Tazmanians have a higher dropout rate than Scots, we need to know this. Facts cannot and should not be a hate crime - and, if the university wished to dispute the statistics, they should provide alternative data. That would have lifted the level of discourse to a science. But saying that such statistics must be ignored as they do not fit in with one's pre-existing notions of the way the world ought to be, is ideology and not political science. Again, enforcing such ideology is a form of indoctrination, not education.

I had made it quite clear why I had published the poster, but both the university and student groups remained 'outraged' that somebody could possibly consider facts over feelings.

After publishing this tweet, I received a letter from the University that read:

> I require you to remove this poster from your Twitter feed immediately as it does not comply with the University's Regulations and is potentially unlawful. You should be aware that the University regularly monitors content posted by students on world wide web and social media.

The poster was not unlawful – and why was the University monitoring content posted by students? Should universities not be encouraging dialogue about political and ideological issues, instead of intensely tracking what every student says and waiting for them to trip over the politically correct line?

On the 12th June 2013, I received further correspondence from the University, this time complaining about tweets I had made that were directed at University lecturer, Dr. Leon Moosavi. In an article on the University of Liverpool website[45] he had, in my opinion, attempted to justify the killing of Lee Rigby. Accordingly, I had felt it necessary to tackle him on the issue.

In a letter between university officials, it was said:

> On 28th May 2013, Mr Buckby's Twitter account was checked and a number of offensive tweets were found, some of which I've quoted from below and a fuller set are also attached as screenshots. He continues to date to post similar tweets.

My Twitter was being monitored. It seemed that the university was out to get me, and as well as the quoted tweets (which you can see below), I received hundreds of pages of documentation and screenshots of my social media pages, where I had spoken about Islam. Many of the tweets also included civilised debate and discussion about Western freedom and the problem of Islamic fundamentalism.

Some of these Tweets are listed below:

- "@Leon_Moosavi belittled problem and blamed it on war. No. Blame it on Islam."
- "If people stop pretending Islam isn't an issue, these attacks couldn't happen."
- "@Leon_Moosavi You're promoting hate, just like you do when you attack remembrance

[45] Moosavi, Leon, "The Liverpool View: Uncomfortable lessons from Woolwich attack," University of Liverpool, 23rd May 2013, http://news.liv.ac.uk/2013/05/23/the-liverpool-view-uncomfortable-lessons-from-woolwich-attack/

day. You're sick. Truly undoubtedly disgusting Leon."

- "Think Islam isn't to blame? You are all part of the problem. You have the blood of millions on your hands."
- "Islam is the only religion that causes this much trouble."
- "Islam teaches violence, conquest and paedophilia. Verifiable facts."

The letter claimed that my calling out Leon Moosavi's views as "disgusting" was in some way problematic for the University. It also acknowledged my remarks about Islam, including my comments about the very real existence of paedophilia in Islam and the constant terror caused by the religion.

It was after receiving this correspondence that the letters, slaps on the wrist and complaining by the University lecturers and administration staff ceased. From here, power was passed to others higher up in the chain of command to take over what had now become the University's concerted efforts to initiate the lengthy process of kicking me out. After attending numerous meetings with University officials, and despite my repeatedly demonstrating to them that I had broken no laws which could provide them with any legal right to kick me out, I eventually grew tired. The University clearly didn't want me; it had already made that quite obvious. But by now I had reached the conclusion that the institutionalised bias and level of teaching was not providing me with the education I had expected. Why should I stay in an institution that hates me, to be taught by people that hate me, and be surrounded by people that hate ideas and discussion?

The University finally decided to remove me from my studies in late 2013, claiming that I had violated Ordinance 17, Clause 2, University Calendar of the University Rules. Regardless of whether this is the case, by kicking me out for my political beliefs and activism on campus, I believe the University has broken the law under Education Act 1981.[46] In Part IV of the 'Miscellaneous' section in the Act, it is stated:

> (1) Every individual and body of persons concerned in the government of any establishment to which this section applies shall take such steps as are reasonably practicable to ensure that freedom of speech within the law is secured for members, students and employees of the establishment and for visiting speakers.

Perhaps the use of the word "reasonable" is what provided the University with belief in its justification for removing me. Clearly there was no reason to suggest I had participated in removing or restricting the freedom of speech of anyone else on campus. Neither had I broken any law. I was always polite, yet I was the one who was regularly attacked (verbally and physically) for disagreeing with the politically correct consensus.

I believe also that my University has violated university guidelines set out by Universities UK. Documents from Universities UK clearly outline the difference between unlawful harassment and freedom of speech, noting "the fact that views are 'offensive' does not in itself mean that the views amount to unlawful harassment.

---

[46] Education Act 1981,
http://www.legislation.gov.uk/ukpga/1981/60/enacted

The document also states that "tolerance and respect for opposing viewpoints are entirely compatible with the fostering of good relations."

It seems to me that nobody at the University of Liverpool has read these guidelines. If they did, they knowingly ignored them. The document also notes that "terrorism is defined as including the use or threat of serious violence against a person or serious damage to property for the purpose of advancing a political, religious or ideological objective."

It's most concerning that even with this obvious definition of terrorism available to university officials, and the numerous death threats I received on campus from people who the university allows to operate on campus, no action was taken. Liverpool anti-fascists regularly threatened to shoot me, wrote articles about how they harassed and chased me, and forced me to obtain a bodyguard to avoid any physical attacks.

For example, if this kind of intimidation and threatening behaviour was projected towards LGBT folk on campus, I imagine the reaction of the University would be wholly different.

These problems I have experienced in university are just the tip of the iceberg. Students all over the Western world are being persecuted by universities for being political and for recognising the serious Marxist bias that trickles from the top down. We are in such a difficult position as students, but the best thing I believe any student can do is stand up against it. Sure, it means they probably won't get a degree – just as I was denied a degree – but what use is a degree these days anyway? Outside of STEM, a degree is nothing but a piece of paper that confirms you've quietly agreed with Marxists for three years.

Students must finally break their silence and start using existing freedom of speech laws to ensure that they get a proper education and are allowed to air their views freely. If only occasionally individual students like myself stand up against this kind of tyranny, then nothing will change. Individuals will be persecuted, and the rest will stay silent and make no change.

I hope that any student reading this considers their future, and the future for their children. The universities are the tools of the multicultural left and Marxists, and without affecting change in universities, our future looks bleak. We can stand for election and fight the Left at the ballot box all we want – but unless people start standing up to the institutions, nothing will ever change.

The NUS "No Platform Policy"

The National Union of Students has enforced a "No Platform Policy" since 1974. In official literature, the NUS claims that the policy is "democratically decided" and that it is voted on at the National Conference each year.[47] The policy currently lists six organisations which it deems "fascist and racist." The NUS states that its policy is designed to "enfranchise freedom of speech and keep students safe."

Amongst the six groups explicitly banned by the NUS from attending university events or speaking on campus are the English Defence League, National Action and the British National Party. They also list two extremist

---

[47] NUS No Platform Policy,
http://www.nusconnect.org.uk/resources/nus-no-platform-policy-f22f

Muslim groups. This has not stopped, however, the innumerable instances of extremist Muslims preaching on British campuses, which is explained in more detail throughout this chapter.

Election of Malia Bouattia

In 2016, a Muslim by the name of Malia Bouattia won a leadership race against incumbent National Union of Students president, Megan Dunn. Bouattia won 50.9% of the vote, and became one of the most divisive leaders in the Union yet. Her victory even came after fifty Jewish student activists had written open letters to the Union expressing their concerns about Bouattia's views. The since-replaced NUS president had previously blasted what she called the "Zionist-led media outlets" in a 2014 speech at the "Gaza and the Palestinian Revolution" gathering[48]. The conference was organized by the "Tricontinental Anti-Imperialist Platform," and was attended by George Galloway – who will be discussed later in this book .

The poster promoting the event featured the faces of Yasser Arafat of the Palestine Libertation Organisation, as well as George Habash from the Popular Front for the Liberation of Palestine, and Hassan Nasrallah of Hezbollah. During her speech at the conference, Bouattia said:

With mainstream Zionist-led media outlets – because once again we're dealing with the population of the global south – resistance is presented as an act of terrorism.

Bouattia's anti-Semitism runs deep. She has

---

[48] "NUS President Malia Bouattia on 'Zionist Led Media Outlets'," The Daily Mail Video, http://www.dailymail.co.uk/video/news/video-1284665/Malia-Bouattia-speaks-Zionist-led-media-outlets.html

previously claimed that Birmingham, an English city with a large immigrant population, is "something of a Zionist outpost."[49]

Before being elected as president of the NUS, Bouattia had spent two years as the Black Students' Officer for the NUS. She was famously involved with the rejection of a motion to condemn the acts of violence and terrorism committed by ISIS. The motion had been proposed by Clifford Fleming and Daniel Cooper, along with the International Students Officer, Shreya Paudel. It called on members of the NUS to "condemn the IS and support Kurdish forces fighting against it, while expressing no confidence or trust in the US military intervention."

This motion was passed by the Scottish National Union of Students, while Bouattia and her Black Students' Officer opposed the motion. Her opposition was then supported by members of the National Executive Committee. Bouattia explained her opposition to the motion, saying:

> We recognise that condemnation of ISIS appears to have become a justification for war and blatant Islamophobia. This rhetoric exacerbates the issue at hand and in essence is a further attack on those we aim to defend.

Bouattia has even taken swipes at critics of CAGE, a London-based organization that claims to empower communities who are impacted by the War on Terror. She opposed plans by former president Megan Dunn to end the

---

[49] "Malia Bouattia stands by Birmingham 'Zionist Outpost' comment," Jewish News, 28th September 2016, http://jewishnews.timesofisrael.com/malia-bouattia-stands-by-birmingham-zionist-outpost-comment/

relationship between CAGE and the NUS. The plans were proposed after former Prime Minister David Cameron accused CAGE of being an extremist group[50], and an investigation by The Daily Mail discovered that the organization had been involved in at least thirteen university events during 2015.[51]

After the media exposed Bouattia's views, the NUS president went on a tirade against the press and claimed that political activists were being "demonized." This, coming from a woman who was elected by more than 50% of students across the country. That NUS election showed that students who refuse to condemn ISIS, who believe the press is controlled by Zionists, and who want the "racist" police force to be scrapped[52] can still be supported by thousands of young people and be elected their president. A woman who has shared platforms with Islamic extremists, and who espouses views that would be deemed unforgivable by British students if they were said by a white man, told a Guardian reporter[53] that she believes she was "vilified." If anything, Bouattia was a beneficiary of a Paradoxical Alliance which is lobotomising British students.

[50] Gani, Aisha, "Cage 'seeking legal advice' on whether it was defamed by David Cameron," The Guardian, 22nd July 2015, https://www.theguardian.com/politics/2015/jul/22/cage-seeks-legal-advice-on-whether-it-was-defamed-by-david-cameron

[51] "Hate-filled extremists warping young minds," The Daily Mail, 8th January 2016, http://www.dailymail.co.uk/debate/article-3389747/DAILY-MAIL-COMMENT-Hate-filled-extremists-warping-young-minds.html

[52] Fielding, James, "Students' union boss says we should scrap our racist police forces," The Express, 24th April 2016, http://www.express.co.uk/news/uk/663843/National-Union-Student-boss-scrap-racist-police-forces

[53] Aitkenhead, Decca, "NUS president Malia Bouattia: 'Political activists are being demonised'," The Guardian, 18th September 2016, https://www.theguardian.com/education/2016/sep/18/nus-president-malia-bouattia-political-activists-are-being-demonised

Universities Caught Promoting Muslim Extremists

Despite being home to the Women Students, Black Students, and LGBT+ Students campaigns, the NUS has become notoriously lax on its vetting procedures when it comes to Muslim guest speakers. Regardless of its 'No Platform Policy' for hateful and racist organisations and figures [the NUS even campaigned against famous feminist Germaine Greer after she said transwomen were not really women], and its rejection of a British culture society which I had attempted to set up during my time at the University of Liverpool, the Union has hosted a plethora of terrorist sympathisers and Muslim extremists.

In September 2015, the NUS came under fire after it was revealed they had invited Moazzam Begg, the outreach director for CAGE, to speak at multiple events being hosted by the Union.[54] Begg had previously admitted to attending Afghanistan training camps, and as a representative of an CAGE he had shown he was still willing to associate with extremists. The research director for CAGE, Asim Qureshi, said during a press conference[55] that a British Arab who worked with the Islamic State in Syria was a "beautiful young man." Known as Jihadi John, but born Muhammad Jassim Abdulkarim Olayan al-Dhafiri, the Muslim terrorist was killed during a drone strike in Raqqa.

In January 2016, an investigation by The Daily Mail found that an extremist Islamic Cleric by the name of Fadel

---

[54] "Moazzam Begg to speak at NUS-organised event tour," Student Rights, 3rd September 2015,
http://www.studentrights.org.uk/article/2299/moazzam_begg_to_speak_at_nus_organised_event_tour_update_nus_statement_
[55] "Islamic State: 'Jihadi John' named as Mohammed Emwazi," BBC News, 26th February 2015, http://www.bbc.co.uk/news/av/world-middle-east-31642385/is-jihadi-john-named-in-45-secs

Soliman had been touring British universities, completely unchallenged[56]. Soliman had spoken at five university events in 2015, where he had encouraged Muslim students and attendees to watch his online sermons. In the online videos, Soliman encouraged the beating of women, and presented a case for polygamy and sex slavery under Islam. The same investigation revealed that MEND had participated in at least ten university events in 2015.

In 2015 Islamophile David Cameron was forced to speak out against the ongoing invitations to extremist Muslims by British universities and the NUS. Owing to the overwhelmingly leftist NUS and universities continuing to invite hate preachers, terrorists, and extremists to speak on campus, the Conservative government's Extremism Taskforce found itself obligated to take action. In a public statement, Prime Minister David Cameron said:

All public institutions have a role to play in rooting out and challenging extremism. It is not about oppressing free speech or stifling academic freedom, it is about making sure that radical views and ideas are not given the oxygen they need to flourish. Schools, universities and colleges, more than anywhere else, have a duty to protect impressionable young minds and ensure that our young people are given every opportunity to reach their potential. That is what our one nation government is focused on delivering.

---

[56] Osborne, Lucy, "'It's fine to hit a wife who doesn't please you': What Islamic cleric is telling students as he tours British universities unchallenged...and he's not alone," The Daily Mail, 9th January 2016, http://www.dailymail.co.uk/news/article-3391194/Speaker-tells-students-s-fine-hit-wife-doesn-t-string-extremists-touring-British-universities-unchallenged.html

The Universities Minister, Jo Johnson, also intervened, writing to the National Union of Students and reminding them of their responsibilities for preventing radicalization. He wrote:

> Universities represent an important arena for challenging extremist views. It is important there can be active challenge and debate on issues relating to counter terrorism and provisions for academic freedom are part of the Prevent guidance for universities and colleges. It is my firm view that we all have a role to play in challenging extremist ideologies and protecting students on campus. Ultimately, the Prevent strategy is about protecting people from radicalisation. It is therefore disappointing to see overt opposition to the Prevent programme…The legal duty that will be placed on universities and colleges highlights the importance that the government places on this.

The intervention by the Conservative government was interesting for two reasons. First of all, the Conservative government elected in 2015 was not by any means strong on the issue of Islam or Jihad, as was explained in the Politics and Islam chapter of this book. For David Cameron to step in shows just how serious the problem with British universities has become. Some seventy events that involved extremist Muslim preachers occurred on campus in 2014,[57] and a further report showed that twenty-seven university

---

[57] Whitehead, Tom, "British universities that give the floor to extremist speakers are named and shamed," The Telegraph, 17th September 2015, http://www.telegraph.co.uk/education/universityeducation/11870429/British-universities-that-give-the-floor-to-extremist-speakers-are-named-and-shamed.html

events invited radical speakers in just four months in 2016.[58] This was despite Cameron's intervention with legislation that required universities to comply with 'Prevent', a Government programme designed to tackle extremism.

Secondly, Cameron's intervention was interesting as it confirmed the government's commitment to silencing anyone who is concerned about the growing threat of Islam. The official statement by the Prime Minister made no reference to Islamism, extremist Islam, or Muslims. Instead, it explicitly called for universities to "root out" and "challenge" extremism, and to make sure that "radical views and ideas are not given the oxygen they need to flourish."

Neglecting Their "Equality" Credentials

Despite bragging about its Black Students, Women Students and LGBT+ Students societies, the National Union of Students continues to pander to extremists who threaten the minorities they wish to protect. By focusing its efforts on banning what they call "fascist" organisations and individuals, the Union ignores the quite obvious problem of radical Muslims whom are not only being invited to speak to the NUS, but are running it.

Every university in Britain has an Equality and Diversity department. Universities UK, a body that helps shape higher education policy, helps universities maintain their equality credentials. The group established a taskforce in September 2015 to assist universities in responding to hate

---

[58] Flood, Rebecca, "Red-carpets laid out for Islam hate preachers at universities and NO-ONE challenges them," The Express, 2nd April 2016, http://www.express.co.uk/news/uk/657609/Britain-s-universities-hosting-extremist-speakers

crime, harassment, and gender-based violence.[59] This is a gigantic industry in the British education system, and yet setting up an official university society that celebrates British culture is seemingly impossible.

My tale is not unique. Students are being silenced by the universities and the National Union of Students all the time. It is clear that university officials, the British government, and the National Union of Students are interested more in perpetuating political ideology than they are in providing an education. It is also clear that political indoctrination is working, when over 50% of students vote to elect an anti-Semitic extremist as their president. This has been going on for decades, and existed long before the "safe space" culture that has become famous in the United States. A long march through our institutions has rendered our universities weak, cowardly, politically motivated, and inconsistent.

---

[59] Universities UK, "Inclusion, equality and diversity",http://www.universitiesuk.ac.uk/policy-and-analysis/Pages/inclusion-equality-diversity.aspx

CHAPTER FOUR
Responses to Terrorism

With each terrorist incident, we see a frightening pattern; Muslims violently attack the West, all the while boldly screaming their religious motivations in the middle of the act and naming their organizations "Islamic"- and the multicultural establishment rushes to protect the reputation of Islam. To the average viewer, the violently attacked West and its allegedly well-meaning institutions defending the source of these attacks must seem increasingly paradoxical and confusing. To help us understand the nature of the players in the Paradoxical Alliance, this chapter will explore the reactions by the police, politicians, left-wing activists, multiculturalists, and pressure groups to the three biggest Islamic attacks in British history.

The 7/7 Bombings

On July 7th 2005 a number of coordinated suicide bomb attacks took place in central London. The general public was targeted and terrorists chose to detonate their explosives on public transport systems. On the morning of July 7th three bombs were detonated in quick succession aboard underground trains throughout London. Soon after a fourth bomb was detonated on a London bus as it passed by Tavistock Square.

The Islamic terrorists used homemade, organic peroxide-based bombs that had been stored in their backpacks, and in their efforts, killed fifty-two people and injured more than seven hundred. The 7/7 bombings were Great Britain's first ever Islamic suicide attack, and despite so many people being killed by Muslims with a clear motive, the politicians, the media and the Left-wing multiculturalist activists invented some of the most common responses to terrorism that we still hear some twelve years later.

Within hours of the attack a website called 'We're Not Afraid!' was launched. The site was designed to give users from all over the world the opportunity to show that they are not intimidated by the attacks. Thousands of images were added to the website and it soon received so much traffic from an adoring press that the site buckled under the pressure. Amusingly, a similar site, more aptly titled 'We're Shitting Ourselves!' was launched around the same time.

Ken Livingstone, the then Mayor of London, delivered a speech which addressed both the bombers and those who inspired them.[60] As well as echoing the message of "We're Not Afraid," Livingstone discussed the motive behind the attack and ignored any Islamic influence, claiming: "That isn't an ideology, it isn't even a perverted faith, it is just indiscriminate attempt at mass murder." Livingstone even condemned the attacks as "cowardly" and addressed the terrorists directly, explaining that "however many you kill, you will fail."

And yet, that day the London Underground ground to a halt. All London buses were sent back to their depots for security checks. Major Network Rail stations in London closed and a majority of national rail services began terminating outside of London. The city's landmarks were closed to the public, the Houses of Parliament and Buckingham Palace were sealed off, and worst of all, the families of fifty-two people went home that night having lost

---

[60] Stone, Jon, "7/7 bombings: Ken Livingstone's speech from Singapore," The Independent, 7th July 2015, http://www.independent.co.uk/news/uk/home-news/ken-livingstones-speech-77-bombings-from-singapore-speak-to-those-come-to-london-10370832.html

loved ones. Seven hundred people were sent to hospital with serious wounds and Great Britain was changed forever. The only people that failed that day were British politicians and the London elite who considered multiculturalism their great strength.

The Hypocrisy of Ken Livingstone

Ken Livingstone has long been a prime player in the Paradoxical Alliance. A socialist, Labour Party politician who served as leader of the Greater London Council from 1981 until it was abolished in 1986, he went on to become the Mayor of London in the year 2000 until 2008. Livingstone was also a Labour Party Member of Parliament for Brent East from 1987 until 2001, and he is famous for identifying as a 'democratic socialist' together with working with far-left politicians such as former London Member of Parliament, George Galloway.

In his second term as Mayor of London, Ken Livingstone's powers were expanded. As well as expanding his policies on the environment and transport, Livingstone set about openly discussing civil rights issues. In 2007, two years after the London attacks, Livingstone marked the 40th anniversary of the decriminalisation of homosexuality in the New Statesman.[61] In his essay, he reaffirmed his commitment to "ensuring our city retains its reputation as a welcoming and safe place for lesbian and gay people to live in and visit."

---

[61] Livingstone, Ken, "Ken Livingstone on gay rights," New Statesman, 20th July 2007, http://www.newstatesman.com/politics/2007/07/lesbian-gay-livingstone-london

He continued:

> I am determined that London continues to lead the way for lesbian, gay, bisexual and trans equality. This year I published the most comprehensive action plan on sexual orientation equality produced in the public sector. However, we also need continued vigilance to tackle inequality and discrimination. This means ongoing work with the police to combat homophobic hate crime and discrimination in the capital and working closely with campaigning organisations such as Stonewall as well as community groups representing London's diverse LGBT community.

Fast-forward five years and Livingstone's attempt to woo the Muslim voters of London saw him promising to make the city a 'beacon' of Islam. Speaking at the North London Central Mosque, otherwise known as the Finsbury Park Mosque, Livingstone promised that, if elected, he would "educate Londoners about Islam." [62] Specifically, Livingstone said:

> I want to spend the next four years making sure that every non-Muslim in London knows and understands [Muhammad's] words and message. That will help to cement our city as a beacon that demonstrated the meanings of the words of the Prophet.

It is evident that Livingstone's response to the Islamic terror attacks on the 7th July 2005 was to appease, appease and appease some more. Not only did he backtrack on his

---

[62] Kern, Soeren, "I Will Make London a Beacon of Islam," Gatestone Institute, 23rd March 2012,
https://www.gatestoneinstitute.org/2967/ken-livingstone-london-islam

commitments to gays and lesbians by promising to make England's capital city a 'beacon' with a religion that stones them to death, he did so at one of the most hard-line mosques in the country. The Finsbury Park Mosque has drawn international attention and criticism owing to its links to terrorism. The mosque has also been host to several extremist Muslim preachers, and in 1996 it installed Abu Hamza al-Masri as its imam. In 2004, the Egyptian cleric was arrested by the British Police when the United States requested that he be extradited in order to face charges. In 2006, a British court found him guilty of inciting violence, and in 2012 he was extradited to the United States where he faced terrorism charges. Hamza was found guilty of eleven charges of terrorism which resulted in a life imprisonment sentence.

No Such 'Backlash' Following the 7/7 Bombings

Scaremongering about a potential 'anti-Muslim backlash' was prevalent in the media after the July 7th attacks. According to a Guardian/ICM poll performed in July 2005,[63] two thirds of Muslims were considering leaving the UK owing to fears of an anti-Muslim backlash. The poll also showed that tens of thousands of Muslims in Britain had experienced 'increased Islamophobia.' Twenty percent of Muslims polled said that they or a family member had experienced anti-Muslim abuse since the attacks.

The reality, however, was much different. In a Daily Mail article published on the 4th December 2006,[64] it was

---

[63] ICM Research, Muslim Poll, July 2005,
http://image.guardian.co.uk/sys-
files/Politics/documents/2005/07/26/Muslim-Poll.pdf
[64] Doughty, Steve, "Race crime backlash after 7/7 did not materialise, admits DPP," 4th December 2006,

reported that the Director of Public Prosecutions (DPP) had said British Muslims did not in fact suffer a backlash of abuse in the wake of the London bombings. In the month of the attack, only twelve individuals were prosecuted for religious hatred in England and Wales, and only six of those cases were directed at Muslims because of the London bombings. DPP Kenneth Macdonald QC said in December 2006 that the fears of a large rise of offences 'appear to be unfounded.' He explained:

> After the 7th July bombings it was feared that there would be a significant backlash against the Muslim community and that we would see a large rise in religiously aggravated offences.

He continued, "Although there were more cases in July 2005 than for any other month, this did not continue into August and overall in 2005/6 there was an increase of nine cases compared to the previous year."

The year 2005 saw a 28% increase in racially aggravated offences being brought to the courts, but it did not represent an increase in the number of incidents taking place. Instead, according to the Crown Prosecution Service, the greater determination on the part of both police and persecutors meant that more incidents were being reported and taken to the courts.

These findings showed that despite media hysteria about an "anti-Muslim backlash," the British people had remained their moderate, tolerant selves and simply accepted that terror attacks were the new normal.

---

http://www.dailymail.co.uk/news/article-420469/Race-crime-backlash-7-7-did-materialise-admits-DPP.html

Leftist/Muslim Peace Vigil

In the wake of the attacks a vigil was held in London. Anti-war, leftist protestors joined forces with British Muslims to send a 'message of commiseration' to the victims and their families[65]. The vigil was held just meters away from the scenes of the 7/7 bus explosion and hundreds of people from the Muslim Association of Britain and the Stop the War Coalition attended to show their support. Wearing black ribbons, attendees were greeted by Member of Parliament George Galloway, the future leader of the Labour Party Jeremy Corbyn, as well as a number of campaigners and artists. Dr Azzam Tamimi, a British Palestinian academic who was also an executive member of the Muslims Association of Britain, gave a speech.

Tamimi exclaimed that the attack was not directed at a certain creed or race, but was an attack on every Londoner. Speaking to the BBC, he explained that Muslims "need to kill the ideology behind this, that justifies the killing of innocents." He also claimed that the attacks were "anti-Islamic" and the government needed pressure to change its policy on Iraq.

However, in November of the previous year Tamimi gave an interview on BBC's Hardtalk where he explained that he would be willing to sacrifice himself if he had the opportunity.[66] He also told the programme that sacrificing his own life for Palestine would be a "noble cause" and that it would be a "straight way to pleasing my God." Tamimi also said in an interview with Spanish newspaper La

---

[65] Browning, Anna, "Vigil sends 'message of commiseration'," BBC News, 10th July 2005, http://news.bbc.co.uk/1/hi/uk/4668373.stm
[66] "Dr Azzam Al-Tamimi," BBC News, 5th November 2004, http://news.bbc.co.uk/1/hi/programmes/hardtalk/3985403.stm

Vanguardia that he admires the Taliban because "they are courageous."

The Murder of Lee Rigby

On May 22nd 2013 an off-duty soldier named Lee Rigby was walking in Wellington Street, Woolwich, when he was suddenly attacked by two men. Two Muslims, Michael Adebowale and Michael Adebolajo, killed him in broad daylight. As they stabbed him with knives and mutilated his body with a cleaver, the two murderers shouted the eternal Muslim war-cry, "Allahu Akbar." The attackers dragged Lee Rigby into the road, whilst onlookers could do nothing but watch as the young man died. In a YouTube clip taken moments after the murder, one of the assailants explains that he killed Lee Rigby because Islam demanded it, and that "you and your children will be next."

As chief spokesperson for the Paradoxical Alliance, British Prime Minister David Cameron quickly told the House of Commons that the killing was a "betrayal of Islam." Specifically, he said:

> What happened on the streets of Woolwich shocked and sickened us all. It was a despicable attack on a British soldier who stood for our country and our way of life and it was too a betrayal of Islam and of the Muslim communities who give so much to our country. There is nothing in Islam that justifies acts of terror and I welcome, too, the spontaneous condemnation of this attack from mosques and Muslim community organisations right across our country. We will not be cowed by terror, and terrorists who seek to divide us will only make us stronger and more united in our resolve to defeat them.

And, not to be outdone, London Mayor Boris Johnson suggested the incident was the result of the "warped mind-set" of the two killers. Specifically, Johnson said that neither Islam nor UK foreign policy are to blame for the mutilation and killing of one of our British soldiers in a busy street. This is despite there being more than one-hundred verses in the Qur'an that call followers of Islam to war with infidels.

Anti-Muslim 'Backlash' Post-Woolwich

As with the 7/7 bombings, those same concerns of an anti-Muslim backlash were announced after the murder of Lee Rigby.

According to Fiyaz Mughal, the founder of Faith Matters and Tell MAMA (Measuring Anti-Muslim Attacks), the events in Woolwich "acted as a catalyst for anti-Muslim sentiment, resulting in a wave of attacks, harassment, and hate-filled speech against Muslims as a generalised category." In an article published at Left Foot Forward,[67] Mughal claimed that in the week following the murder of Lee Rigby, an "unprecedented number of incidents have been reported, with over 200 cases so far, and more coming in every day."

Left Foot Forward is a left-wing British publication that claims to provide "evidence-based analysis of British politics." It is edited by Niamh Ní Mhaoileoin, a blogger and activist who served as the Press Officer for the 'Women's Equality Party' between September 2015 and December 2015.

---

[67] Mughal, Fiyaz, "Anti-Muslim incidents and the Woolwich attack: an initial appraisal," Left Foot Forward, 31st May 2013, http://leftfootforward.org/2013/05/anti-muslim-incidents-and-the-woolwich-attack-an-initial-appraisal/

In Mughal's article for Left Foot Forward, he further claimed that "one of the most obvious indicators has been the rise in street harassment of Muslims – unprovoked, opportunistic attacks from strangers as Muslims go about their lives." This was challenged, however, in a June 2013 article[68] by Andrew Gilligan in The Telegraph. In the article entitled "The truth about the 'wave of attacks on Muslims' after Woolwich murder," Gilligan challenged Mughal's claims and called out the BBC for having accepted the claims without question.

Gilligan outlined how the basis of Mughal's claims were the 212 anti-Muslim incidents which had been logged through Tell Mama after the Woolwich murder. In The Sunday Telegraph, Tell Mama confirmed that out of 120 of these incidents, some 57%, took place online, meaning that the organisation had been logging Tweets and Facebook posts as 'anti-Muslim incidents.' Furthermore, Gilligan explained how Tell Mama had no written definition of what it considered an anti-Muslim incident. Gilligan also said that the British taxpayer was spending £214,000 per year on the outfit.

The government-funded organisation claims that its caseworkers "carefully handle each report as it comes in, to determine whether it can be verified and justified as an anti-Muslim incident," but Gilligan further detailed how 16% of the 212 post-Woolwich anti-Muslim incidents were yet to be verified. Just 8% of the 212 incidents reported actually involved Muslims being physically targeted. Gilligan rightly

---

[68] Gilligan, Andrew, "The truth about the 'wave of attacks on Muslims' after Woolwich murder," The Telegraph, 1st June 2013, http://www.telegraph.co.uk/news/uknews/terrorism-in-the-uk/10093568/The-truth-about-the-wave-of-attacks-on-Muslims-after-Woolwich-murder.html

stated in his article that the main victim of this attack was Drummer Lee Rigby, and that "in overhyping the backlash, some in the Muslim community are playing right into the hands of his killers."

As well as receiving £214,000 in public money, Tell Mama gained the support of Mark David Oakley, a Church of England priest, The Canon Chancellor of St Paul's Cathedral in London, and a former Archdeacon of Germany and Northern Europe. In a sign that the Church of England has become fully committed to multiculturalism, and to support ideologies that fundamentally oppose Britain's state religion, Oakley became a patron of Tell Mama. Oakley is also an ambassador for a Leeds-based charity called Stop Hate UK, which claims to be dedicated to "raising awareness and understanding of discrimination and Hate Crime, encouraging its reporting and supporting the individuals and communities it affects." The charity operates a Lesbian, Gay and Bisexual helpline, a Transgender helpline, and a general 'Stop Hate' helpline. The same organisation reported that, following the UK's vote to leave the European Union in June 2016, there was a growth in 'hate incidents' throughout the country.[69]

In a Spring 2013 newsletter,[70] Stop Hate UK condemned the killing of Lee Rigby in two sentences. The condemnation was followed by multiple paragraphs that explained how, after the killing, action must be taken to stop "tensions from escalating." The newsletter also went on to condemn demonstrations that took place in Woolwich after

---

[69] "EU Referendum: Hate Incident Reporting post 'Brexit'," Stop Hate UK, http://www.stophateuk.org/wp-content/uploads/2016/08/Stop-Hate-UK_EU-Referendum-Report_V2a_Email.pdf
[70] "Stop Hate UK Newsletter Spring/Summer 2013", Stop Hate UK, http://www.cnet.org.uk/_library/downloads/StopHateUKNewsletter_Spring_2013.pdf

the murder which were designed to raise awareness of the threat of Islam in London and Britain as a whole.

Even British police perpetuated the "anti-Muslim backlash" narrative with coppers in Scotland pledging to halt any backlash following the Woolwich incident.[71]

The 2017 Westminster Attack

On the 22nd March 2017, a man driving a 4x4 across Westminster Bridge mounted the kerb and mowed down more than fifty people. After crashing into the perimeter fence of Westminster Palace, the man left the vehicle and stabbed an unarmed police officer to death. In just eighty-two seconds, the perpetrator, Khalid Massood, killed five people.

I was in London at the time and immediately hailed a taxi to the scene of the attack when I heard the breaking news. Just meters away from dead bodies, the media were gathered trying to get their best look, and upon recognising Tommy Robinson - whom I was with at the time – began asking questions about "far right terrorism."

One Asian reporter laughed at Tommy as he explained that the attack was clearly inspired by Al Qaeda's magazine 'Inspire.' The booklet, which was reportedly downloaded by 50,000 British Muslims over three months in 2015,[72] explains how to perform low-tech terror attacks using nothing more than a vehicle and a knife.

---

[71] Scott, David, "Scots cops in pledge to foil anti-Muslim backlash," The Express, 24th May 2013, http://www.express.co.uk/news/uk/402068/Scots-cops-in-pledge-to-foil-anti-Muslim-backlash

[72] Wilkinson, Matt, "Bomb guide read 4,000 times in UK," The Sun, 18th January 2015,

The Prime Minister's Response

Echoing the statements made in the wake of both the 7/7 bombings and the Lee Rigby attack, Prime Minister Theresa May said in a speech after the Westminster Attack that Britain will "all move forward together, never giving in to terror."

After chairing a COBRA (Cabinet Office Briefing Room A) meeting, the Prime Minister said to the people of Britain:

> Tomorrow morning, Parliament will meet as normal. We will come together as normal. And Londoners - and others from around the world who have come here to visit this great City - will get up and go about their day as normal. They will board their trains, they will leave their hotels, they will walk these streets, they will live their lives.

In Parliament, May was asked by Conservative Member of Parliament Michael Tomlinson whether she thought it appropriate to label this as "Islamic terrorism." Tomlinson asked: "Will the Prime Minister agree with me that what happened was not Islamic, just as the murder of Airey Neave was not Christian, and that in fact both are perversions of religion?"

Mrs May responded: "I absolutely agree, and it is wrong to describe this as Islamic terrorism. It is Islamist terrorism. It is a perversion of a great faith."

---

https://www.thesun.co.uk/archives/news/13230/bomb-guide-read-4000-times-in-uk/

The 'Anti-Muslim Backlash'

Just as with previous Islamic terror attacks in Britain, the police, media and politicians were keen to express their concern about an "anti-Muslim backlash." The Guardian reported on the 24th March that Muslims in a mosque linked to Khalid Masood feared an "anti-Islam backlash."[73] The Guardian spoke to worshippers at the al-Tawhid mosque in Leyton, East London. Reporters Helen Pidd and Harriet Sherwood explained how the "atmosphere was nervous" as the mosque volunteers unlocked their doors before welcoming worshippers. One such worshipper, who called himself Abdullah, explained how he was saddened to not be greeted by a colleague at work.

He said: "She wouldn't make eye contact. I was hurt. They think, Abdullah is a Muslim, maybe he is a terrorist, too. It's very depressing."

The fear of any real 'anti-Muslim backlash' was, however, unfounded. Even Fiyaz Mughal's Tell Mama was forced to admit there was no such backlash.[74] On March 29th, the Tell Mama website reported that "Anti-Muslim hate did not reach high peaks after the Westminster terrorist attacks." The article claimed that the "usual picture has been that after a major terrorist attack, there is a corresponding significant peak and rise in anti-Muslim hatred."

---

[73] Sherwood, Harriet, "Muslims at mosques linked to Khalid Masood fear anti-Islam backlash," The Guardian, 24th March 2017, https://www.theguardian.com/uk-news/2017/mar/24/westminster-attack-khalid-masood-anti-muslim-backlash-mosques-east-london-birmingham
[74] "Anti-Muslim Hate Did Not Reach High Peaks After the Westminster Terrorist Attacks," Tell MAMA, 29th March 2017, https://tellmamauk.org/anti-muslim-hate-not-reach-high-peaks-westminster-terrorist-attacks/

In the wake of this, it was revealed that British Police had actively sought out reports of 'Islamophobia' after the attack.[75] The Acting Metropolitan Police Commissioner, Craig Mackey, did report a 'slight uplift' in Islamophobia after the attack, although an investigation by Breitbart London found that this could have been attributable to authorities encouraging Muslims to come forward with allegations of 'Islamophobic incidents' after the attack. Mackey admitted that the increase was "small, and far smaller than we have seen in previous events."

When contacting the Metropolitan Police press bureau for information about Mackey's claim, Breitbart London found that on the day of the incident, two Islamophobic incidents had been reported by the police. Incidents were also reported in the following days and were reported as follows:

- Thursday: 10 Islamophobic incidents
- Friday: 11 Islamophobic incidents
- Saturday: 5 Islamophobic incidents
- Sunday: 8 Islamophobic incidents
- Monday: 3 Islamophobic incidents

The figures were sent to Breitbart London along with a report which suggested that these reports may not have come from people who truly considered them a victim of an attack or Islamophobic 'incident', but as a result of a 'community engagement plan' that was put in place by authorities. The report described how the authorities identify 'trigger events' that they believe could result in increased hate crime activity.

[75] Montgomery, Jack, "Exclusive: UK Police Sought Out 'Islamophobia' Reports to Claim Rise After Westminster Attack," Breitbart, 30th March 2017, http://www.breitbart.com/london/2017/03/29/uk-police-sought-islamophobia-reports-claim-rise-westminster-attack/

When a 'trigger event' occurs, the New Scotland Yard says, authorities instigate a community engagement plan which "ensures those in communities who may be victims of hate crime know that we will not tolerate this kind of crime and that we encourage them to report this to the police."

The statement also revealed the Metropolitan Police's effort to increase hate crime recordings, in order to stay within the guidelines of government policy, by employing some 900 hate crime specialists. This move came after government policy was implemented which focused on increasing the reporting of hate crime.[76] The government legislation, entitled 'Action Against Hate: The UK Government's Plan for Tackling Hate Crime', outlines its plans for increasing the reporting of hate crime. Specifically, the legislation sets out the following goal.

> Increasing the reporting of hate crime, through improving the reporting process, encouraging the use of third party reporting and working with groups who may under-report, such as disabled people, Muslim women, the Charedit community, transgender people, Gypsy, Traveller and Roma communities, and new refugee communities. We will work with the Crown Prosecution Service (CPS) to ensure that perpetrators are punished, and to publicise successful prosecutions to encourage people to have the confidence that when they report hate crime, action will be taken.

---

[76]"Action Against Hate: The UK Government's plan for tackling hate crime," July 2016,
https://www.gov.uk/government/uploads/system/uploads/attachment_d ata/file/543679/Action_Against_Hate_-
_UK_Government_s_Plan_to_Tackle_Hate_Crime_2016.pdf

The legislation speaks quite generally about increasing the reporting of hate crimes, while the Metropolitan Police explicitly outline how they encourage the reporting of hate crimes after what they call 'trigger events.' While legislation may be innocently suggesting that people do not feel comfortable coming forward about hate crime incidents, the Metropolitan Police appear to be deliberately seeking Islamophobic incidents, or other hate crimes, after terrorist attacks and other 'trigger events.' This purposely skews data and implies either great incompetency within the Metropolitan Police, or a concerted effort to create a narrative which suggests hate crimes soar after terrorist attacks take place. This is particularly worrying as it aids the agenda of the politicians and the press to remove focus from the source of these terror attacks in Europe, and to instead perpetuate the notion that the British public are inherently hateful and intolerant of ethnic minorities.

By creating and perpetuating this narrative of victimhood across the country, the Metropolitan Police and British lawmakers are demonising their own people and constituents, and emboldening Islamic fundamentalists who use the victim card to push further government schemes, bills and programs to provide funding and support for Islamic institutions in Britain. This Paradoxical Alliance sees the British government and elected officials aiding people and institutions who will, in a matter of a generation or two, replace them entirely.

MEND's Response

In the wake of the Westminster attack, Muslim Engagement and Development (MEND), whose influence over British politicians was discussed in chapter two, appointed a new director. In April 2017, MEND appointed an Islamist who had previously claimed that killing British soldiers was 'justified', as a director of the organisation. The new head of community development and engagement at MEND, Azad Ali, also weighed in on the terrorist attack at Westminster.

The Daily Mail reported that, in a Facebook post, Ali claimed that Masood should be treated as a "lone wolf" and that it was "not terrorism", even after it had emerged that multiple arrests had been made in connection to the incident.[77] In 2010 Ali lost a libel case which he brought against the Mail newspapers. Ali objected to the claims that he was a "hardline Islamic extremist who supports the killing of British and American soldiers in Iraq by fellow Muslims." He lost the case on the basis that he had appeared to support the killing of British and American soldiers in a blog post. Ali has also admitted to having attended talks by Abu Qatada,[78] a Salafi cleric with links to terrorist organisations, and who has previously denied that the Mumbai attacks of 2008 were terrorism[79]. During his time working as a civil servant in the Treasury, Ali wrote on his personal blogs that he considered the attacks by members of Lashkar-e-Taiba in Mumbai were not terrorism. He said this while sitting on a Whitehall counter-terrorism panel, which at the time provided information and advice to the director of public prosecutions, Keir Starmer.

---

[77] Robinson, Martin, "Islamist who claimed killing British soldiers was 'justified' becomes director of a controversial Muslim pressure group with influence over Westminster," The Daily Mail, 10th April 2017, http://www.dailymail.co.uk/news/article-4396832/Islamist-head-Muslim-pressure-group.html#ixzz4dvMd6tQU
[78] "Abu Qatada row could make him a 'cause celebre for extremists'," BBC News, 14th February 2012, http://www.bbc.co.uk/news/uk-england-london-17034299
[79] "UK civil servant says 26/11 not terror attack," The Indian Express, 2nd November 2009, http://archive.indianexpress.com/news/uk-civil-servant-says-2611-not-terror-attack/536019/

Not only does Azad Ali influence decisions made by British politicians through his work at MEND, and deny the nature of terror attacks in Britain, but his influence dates back many years to the time when he walked the corridors of Whitehall and had the ear of influential British politicians.

This seems to be a pattern in British politics. Politicians from both the Labour Party and the Conservative Party appear willing to appease Islamic radicals by not only hiring them, but hiring them and putting them in positions of influence over issues like terrorism. For a man like Azad Ali, who has lost libel cases over his support for the killing of British and American troops, to be advising government officials on matters of terrorism is insanity on a magnitude that a vast majority of normal people cannot quite fathom. In the world of politics, and the Paradoxical Alliance however, it is all perfectly normal.

The Qur'an Calls for Terror

When British politicians deny that terror attacks are not Islamic, or are a perversion of a great faith, they are expressing a deep ignorance of Islam's history, and its holy book the Qur'an. Politicians such as Theresa May, David Cameron, Ken Livingstone and more are concerned only about their ability to be elected, or to avoid a negative backlash in the press. Should a journalist even catch a whiff of a politician admitting that religion could in fact be a driving factor behind Islamic attacks, the rape of young girls or the oppression of grown women, politicians quiver at the knees at their impending doom. Headlines slamming politicians for Islamophobia or bigotry are career-ending, at least they are if you are a member of 'inclusive' political parties like the Conservatives, Labour or the Liberal Democrats. Ironically, headlines accusing politicians of Islamophobia would have quite the opposite effect for any truly patriotic politician who was vying for the support of the average working Brit. That is, the average working Brit who is forced to live within Islamic ghettoes that the politicians created in the first place and then later went on to forget about.

The Qur'an explicitly calls for terror, and under the rules of our governing Paradoxical Alliance, these verses must be ignored or interpreted to a point where they become unrecognisable. Literal interpretation has been the foundation of the legal system in the West since the very beginning, and only with the Qur'an is this considered unreasonable. The Islamic holy book must be the single most misunderstood thing ever written because despite the following verses which clearly call for acts of terrorism, our leaders tell us that we're just not reading it right.

Qur'an 3:151: "Soon shall We cast terror into the hearts of the Unbelievers, for that they joined companions with Allah, for which He had sent no authority."

Qur'an 4:74: "Let those fight in the way of Allah who sell the life of this world for the other. Whoso fighteth in the way of Allah, be he slain or be he victorious, on him We shall bestow a vast reward."

Qur'an 5:33: "The punishment of those who wage war against Allah and His messenger and strive to make mischief in the land is only this, that they should be murdered or crucified or their hands and their feet should be cut off on opposite sides or they should be imprisoned; this shall be as a disgrace for them in this world, and in the hereafter they shall have a grievous chastisement."

Qur'an 8:12: "I will cast terror into the hearts of those who disbelieve. Therefore strike off their heads and strike off every fingertip of them."

There are 164 verses relating to violence in the cause of Jihad in the Qur'an.[80] These verses speak honestly and openly about military expedition, fighting, punishment and looting. However, when including verses which discuss Muhammad's opinion of those who do not perform Jihad, the rewards for Jihadists, and forms of Jihad outside of violence, there are significantly more than 164.

When Lee Rigby's murderers hacked his head off with a cleaver shouting "Allahu Akbar" and telling us that their religion had instructed them to commit these acts, we must believe them. The Qur'an instructs Muslims to "cast terror into the hearts of those who disbelieve," and this is exactly what we are seeing throughout Europe. Islamic Jihad attacks are almost a daily occurrence.

When the multicultural Left, the politicians and the press ignore the source of these problems – or imply that these terror attacks are caused by mental illness as opposed to religious influence – they are actively welcoming their own destruction. Jihadists do not want a liberal democracy, and neither do Muslims. By giving Muslims a free pass when it comes to terrorism, the multicultural Left is signing its own death warrant. Time and time again opinion polls have shown us that Muslims do not want a liberal democracy, do not want rights for the minorities that the Left purports to defend, and do not want to assimilate into a tolerant Western civilisation.

---

[80] http://www.answering-islam.org/Qur'an/Themes/jihad_passages.html

Twenty-eight percent of British Muslims want Britain to become an Islamic state, and according to the Policy Exchange, 61% of British Muslims want homosexuality punished.[81] Forty percent of British Muslims want Sharia implemented in the United Kingdom,[82] and ¼ of British Muslims believe that the 7/7 bombings were justified.[83] When the Paradoxical Alliance tells us to think again about the source of Islamic terror in Britain, not only are they making our society less safe, but they are putting their own people in danger. A society that is cowed by terrorism, and which is experiencing an Islamic demographic boom, will not be friendly to minorities – and we know this thanks to a plethora of opinion polls taken over the last ten years and the fourteen-hundred years of Islamic history.

---

[81] MacEoin, Denis, "Sharia Law or 'One Law For All?' Civitas: Institute for the Study of Civil Society London, June 2009, http://www.civitas.org.uk/pdf/ShariaLawOrOneLawForAll.pdf
[82] "The latest WikiLeaks revelation: 1 in 3 British Muslim students back killing for Islam and 40% want Sharia law," The Daily Mail, 22nd December 2010, http://www.dailymail.co.uk/news/article-1340599/WikiLeaks-1-3-British-Muslim-students-killing-Islam-40-want-Sharia-law.html
[83] Cosgrove-Mather, Bootie, "Many British Muslims Put Islam First," CBS News, 14th August 2006, http://www.cbsnews.com/news/many-british-muslims-put-islam-first/

CHAPTER FIVE
Qur'an Vs. Magna Carta

To end this half of this book, I'll contrast the Magna Carta with the Qur'an. The Magna Carta (full name Magna Carta Libertatum, which is Medieval Latin for "the Great Charter of the Liberties"), is a charter that has formed the basis of modern English law. The document was originally signed by King John of England in June 1215. It was drafted by the Archbishop of Canterbury, and it set out to guarantee the English people access to justice, and churches a protection of their rights. It also offered protection for barons from being illegally imprisoned, in an attempt to make peace between rebels and the highly unpopular King John. The barons had captured London in May 1215, forcing the King to negotiate and create the charter. What was originally designed to be a peacekeeping effort, however, ultimately formed the basis of modern law, civil liberties, and rights enjoyed not just in England, but across the Atlantic.

The document, written entirely in Latin, originally had 63 clauses. After being amended by monarchs over generations, and through the introduction of other laws, just four clauses remain. These four clauses, however, do a terrific job of defining the freedoms enjoyed in our British culture. By comparing these four clauses with the Qur'an – the holy book that dictates the rules of Islamic society – the Paradoxical Alliance becomes even more clear. When multiculturalists defend Islam, they are defending a theocratic ideology that denies its followers the rights given to us by the Magna Carta.

Clause One

First, that we have granted God, and by this present charter have confirmed for us and our heirs in perpetuity, that the English Church shall be free, and shall have its rights undiminished, and its liberties unimpaired. That we wish this so to be observed, appears from the fact that of our own free will, before the outbreak of the present dispute between us and our barons, we granted and confirmed by charter the freedom of the Church's elections - a right reckoned to be of the greatest necessity and importance to it - and caused this to be confirmed by Pope Innocent III. This freedom we shall observe ourselves, and desire to be observed in good faith by our heirs in perpetuity.

The first clause of the Magna Carta guarantees freedom for the English church. The clause was written specifically to ensure that the king could have no involvement in the church. It also gave the church the right to elect its own leaders. Previously, the king would have appointed these leaders.

This is an early example of the separation of church and state. In the United Kingdom, there is only relative separation of church and state – there is one link between the two which remains to this day, and that comes in the form of the Lords Spiritual. These are spiritual peers who take seats in the House of Lords, the second chamber of Parliament. They have all the same rights as regular peers in the House of Lords, and they wield their power by voting in a bloc on issues that relate to the Church. There are 26 bishops of the Church of England who serve as Lords Spiritual.

The Church of England does have some legal rights and responsibilities when it comes to marriage, and the state does fund some faith schools. Beyond this, however, there is little that the church can do to influence elections or governmental decisions. The state and the monarch, as laid out in the Magna Carta, cannot make decisions about leaders in the church.

This marks an important difference between British culture and Islamic culture. Under Sharia, there is no separation between mosque and state. Sayyib Qutb, an Egyptian author and Islamic theorist, as well as a leading member of the Muslim Brotherhood in the mid-20th century, said "it is an obligation for people to make the Sharia of God that which rules every aspect of every affair of this life."[84] In a book written by 20th century Muslim revivalist Muḥammad Hasan Amāra, entitled Islam and Politics: A Response to the Heresies of the Secularists, the concept of separate state and religion was criticized. Amāra said that "secularism is a school of thought of modern Western Civilisation."[85]

Modern Islamic scholars argue the same thing. Shadi Hamid, the author of Islamic Exceptionalism: How the Struggle Over Islam is Reshaping the World, and a senior fellow of the Brookings Institution, said in 2016 that the Western concept that all religions are the same and have the same goals is fundamentally incorrect. In a Los Angeles Times piece, Hamid outlined how Islam is fundamentally different to Western culture and religion.[86] He also said:

"Differences between Christianity and Islam also are evident in each faith's central figure. Unlike Jesus, who was a dissident, Muhammad was both prophet

---

[84] Qutb, Sayyid, Maʿālim fī al-Ṭarīq, 6th reprint (Beirūt; Cairo: Dar al-Shurūq, 1979), p.47

[85] Amāra, Muḥammad, al-Islām wa al-Sīyāsa: al-Radd ʿala Shubuhāt al-ʿAlmānīyīn, (Cairo: Maktabat al-Shurūq al-Dowlīya, 2008), p.28

[86] Hamid, Shadi, "From burkinis to the Qurʾan: Why Islam isn't like other faiths," Los Angeles Times, 9th September 2016, http://www.latimes.com/opinion/op-ed/la-oe-hamid-islamic-exceptionalism-burkini-20160909-snap-story.html

and politician. And more than just any politician, he was a state-builder as well as a head of state."

These statements are based on the teachings of the Qur'an, as well as the Hadith (reports of words and actions by Muhammed) and Sira (biographies of Muhammed).

Qur'an 4:141 says "...never will Allah grant to the unbelievers a way to triumph over the believers." In a modern, Western democracy, anybody regardless of their faith can stand for election to public office. Under Islam, there must be no way for unbelievers to "triumph" over the believers.

Clause Thirteen

The city of London shall enjoy all its ancient liberties and free customs, both by land and by water. We also will and grant that all other cities, boroughs, towns, and ports shall enjoy all their liberties and free customs.

The thirteenth clause was written to ensure that London, and other cities and towns throughout the country, did not have their rights stripped away by a corrupt king. One such right for London was their ability to elect a mayor. Under Islam, this allocation of authority is not permitted. While a man may rule his household, democratic elections and authority to dictate policy over a people are not allowed.

Qur'an 12:40 explicitly says that Allah is the only source of law or rule. It says "...Allah hath sent down no authority: the command is for none but Allah..."

Islamic scripture and scholars have confirmed throughout history that under Allah, there is no manmade rule or law. Allah has sent down no authority. It is for this reason that much of the Muslim world lives under theocratic rule to this day – unlike in Britain, where there has been a separation of powers for many hundreds of years.

Clause Thirty-Nine and Forty

While clause thirty-nine and forty are not the origin of Habeas Corpus (this came much later), they are often considered an early framework for the introduction of trial by jury and the banning of arbitrary detention.

Clause Thirty-Nine:

> No free man shall be seized or imprisoned, or stripped of his rights or possessions, or outlawed or exiled, or deprived of his standing in any way, nor will we proceed with force against him, or send others to do so, except by the lawful judgment of his equals or by the law of the land.

Clause Forty:

> To no one will we sell, to no one deny or delay right or justice.

The Habeas Corpus Act was passed in Parliament in 1679. The act codified the ancient writ, bringing it into English law. The English were then protected against unlawful detention, and the courts were granted power to determine the legality of any imprisonment. To this day, Habeas Corpus, and the right of a citizen to be tried by a jury of their peers have been exported to most modern democracies. This is not the case in theocratic, Islamic societies.

Under English law for instance, both parties must consent to be married. Forced marriage leads to a multitude of charges, including false imprisonment.[87] Under Sharia, however, a girl may be forced to marry a man chosen by her family. It is for this reason that legislation was introduced and came into force on 16th June 2014 in the United Kingdom, which made forced marriage an offence under section 121 of the Anti-Social Behaviour, Crime and Policing Act 2014.[88] Many laws surrounding false imprisonment and other religion-based crimes have only recently been introduced, as more Sharia courts are established and Muslim immigration increases.

The difference between English law and Sharia also becomes strikingly obvious when comparing the rights of women. Under English law, the testimony of men and women is considered equal. In Qur'an 2:282, which refers to court testimony, it says "And call to witness, from among your men, two witnesses. And if two men be not found then a man and two women." In Qur'an 4:11, which refers to inheritance, it echoes the suggestion that the testimony of a woman is worth half of a man when it says "The male shall have the equal of the portion of two females."

This is further established in Qur'an 2:228, which says "and the men are a degree above them."

Beyond family law matters, the concept of Habeas Corpus is noticeably absent in the Muslim world when one

---

[87] "Honour Based Violence and Forced Marriage," Crown Prosecution Service,
http://www.cps.gov.uk/legal/h_to_k/honour_based_violence_and_force d_marriage/
[88] "Anti-social Behaviour, Crime and Policing ACT 2014," 2014 C.12, Part 10, Section 121,
http://www.legislation.gov.uk/ukpga/2014/12/section/121/enacted

considers the modern slave trade. Human trafficking is rife throughout the Muslim world, with Afghanistan being a prominent source of this criminal activity. Afghanistan is "a source, transit, and destination country for men, women and children subjected to forced labor and sex trafficking" according to the United States Department of State's 2016 Trafficking in Person Report.[89] A study from the International Labour Office in 2004 also showed that out of the million haari families living in Sindh (a province of Pakistan), the majority are living in debt bondage.[90] The United Nations describes this as a form of modern-day slavery.

In Saudi Arabia, where slavery was outlawed in 1962, the practice remains commonplace. The United States State Department continues to report on Saudi Arabia's human trafficking problem[91], and even a leading Islamic theologian from Saudi Arabia has suggested that the rejection of slavery is to be un-Islamic. Sheikh Saleh Al-Fawzan, the author of At-Tawhid, said in a lecture that "slavery is a part of Islam. Slavery is part of jihad, and jihad will remain as long as there is Islam."[92]

---

[89] "Afghanistan: Tier 2 Watch List," Office to Monitor and Combat Trafficking in Persons, 2016 Trafficking in Persons Report, https://www.state.gov/j/tip/rls/tiprpt/countries/2016/258708.htm

[90] H. Hussein, Maliha, "Bonded labour in agriculture: a rapid assessment in Singh and Balochistan Pakistan," International Labour Office, March 2004, http://www.ilo.org/wcmsp5/groups/public/@ed_norm/@declaration/documents/publication/wcms_082026.pdf

[91] "Saudi Arabia (Tier 3)," Office to Monitor and Combat Trafficking in Persons, 2008 Trafficking in Persons Report, https://www.state.gov/j/tip/rls/tiprpt/2008/105389.htm

[92] Pipes, Daniel, "Islamist Calls for Slavery's Legalization," Daniel Pipes Middle East Forum, 7th November 2003, http://www.danielpipes.org/blog/2003/11/saudi-religious-leader-calls-for-slaverys

This sentiment is supported by the actions of Muhammad, who captured, owned, and even sold slaves during his life. There are numerous verses in the Qur'an which endorse and encourage slavery – particularly, sex slavery. One of the most famous verses from the holy book which endorses this comes from Qur'an 33:50, which reads:

> O Prophet! We have made lawful to thee thy wives to whom thou hast paid their dowers; and those (slaves) whom thy right hand possesses out of the prisoners of war whom Allah has assigned to thee.

Through even the most basic of analysis, it is abundantly clear that the values held dear in Western society are fundamentally different to the values in Muslim societies. To this day, the Muslim world practices slavery and turns a blind eye to unlawful imprisonment. It enforces strict theocratic rule, and it rejects manmade law. Whether Islam is compatible in a Western, liberal society should not even be in question. The values put forward under Sharia fly in the face of the values cherished not just by conservatives, but by the Liberals who defend Islam at all costs. Only indoctrination at the most monumental of scales, a scale almost beyond the comprehension, could create a population of people who can ignore the quite obviously paradoxical nature of the alliance between the radical left and Islam.

This Paradoxical Alliance is becoming increasingly noticeable as Islamic attacks increase in frequency, and as freedom of speech is curtailed in the name of religious tolerance. Great Britain may well be the home of many of the freedoms and rights enjoyed by the Western world today, but it could easily become the resting place of those same values if the Paradoxical Alliance is not confronted.

AMERICA

Introduction: America's First War with Islam

America's conflicts with Islam are nearly as old as America itself - and Europe's dates back far longer. It should come as a wakeup call for those blaming Islamic violence on "American imperialism" that our conflict with the Muslim world far predates anything that could be considered as much.

Like most people, you're probably unaware that roughly 1.5 million Europeans and Americans were enslaved in Islamic North Africa between 1530 and 1780.[93] Naturally, that was a political issue at that time.

The Muslim pirates responsible for the enslavement all came from the Barbary Coast - Morocco, Algiers, Tunis, and Tripoli.

In March of 1786, Thomas Jefferson and John Adams made a trip to visit Tripoli's ambassador to London. They asked why it was they attacked American ships and enslaved their people (yes - this is completely hypocritical given the law on slavery in America at the time), given that we had done the Barbary nations "no injury." The response from the ambassador, Sidi Haji Abdrahaman, essentially boiled down to the religious version of "because we can."

Jefferson wrote in a letter to John Jay relaying the exchange:

---

[93] Hitchens, Christopher. "Jefferson Versus the Muslim Pirates." City-Journal, Spring 2007. https://www.city-journal.org/html/jefferson-versus-muslim-pirates-13013.html

The Ambassador answered us that it was founded on the Laws of their Prophet, that it was written in their Koran, that all nations who should not have acknowledged their authority were sinners, that it was their right and duty to make war upon them wherever they could be found, and to make slaves of all they could take as Prisoners, and that every Musselman [Muslim] who should be slain in battle was sure to go to Paradise. [94]

Hardly the kind of response you can blame on American aggression, Islamophobia, or a few bad apples. It was a response which, as the late Christopher Hitchens notes, likely became the moment that Jefferson decided he would make war with the Barbary kingdoms as soon as he commanded America's armed forces. It would be an opportunity to attack what represented two institutions he despised most, state-sponsored religion, and enthroned monarchy, "and it may even be that his famous ambivalences about slavery were resolved somewhat when he saw it practiced by the Muslims," Hitchens speculated.

For years afterward, the American government paid the Barbary nations millions in "tribute" money to guarantee the safe passage of our merchant ships, which continued to grow to the point of consuming 10% of the national budget.

It wasn't until March 1801 that Jefferson became the third President of the United States - and that's when he turned up the heat on our foreign foes. Having long advocated against paying for protection from those they needed it against, instead advocating for war, Jefferson began the First Barbary War just months into his presidency.

---

[94] "American Commissioners to John Jay, 28 March 1786" Founders Online, https://founders.archives.gov/documents/Jefferson/01-09-02-0315.

George Washington and John Adams had also been among those concurring with Jefferson's calls to end the tribute years prior, though Adams believed that America should pay it until we could build up a Navy first.[95]

Once Jefferson was in office, Tripoli's Pasha[96] Yusef Karamanli demanded a tribute of $225,000 from America, which Jefferson refused. In response, Karamanli declared war on America in May by chopping down the American flag present at the U.S. consulate in Tripoli.[97]

His actions were promptly answered with an assault on Barbary forces, crippling one of their most important ships. "The style of the demand admitted but one answer," he would later tell Congress in his annual address - as his actions thus far had been undertaken without congressional approval.

Congress was on board.

In February of 1802, Congress passed an act containing a provision allowing for a permanent presence in the Mediterranean. Its reference to the "Tripolitan Corsairs," like the chopping down of the American flag in Tripoli, amounted to an indirect declaration of war.

For the following three years, Karamanli's call for a tribute to be paid continued, as did the war.

---

[95] I should note that this is in reference to before Jefferson took office, as Washington died before he did.
[96] A rank in the Ottoman Empire typically granted to governors, generals, and dignitaries.
[97] Huff, Elizabeth, Riscilla Roberts, and Richard Roberts. "The First Barbary War." The Thomas Jefferson Foundation. https://www.monticello.org/site/research-and-collections/first-barbary-war.

The most significant victory for the Barbary forces ended up being short lived, when they took the U.S. Philadelphia in October of 1803. The 307-man crew was imprisoned, and the ship was repaired and recommissioned for the use of the Barbary forces. But before they could actually put the ship to use, a U.S. Navy team sailed into Tripoli harbor on the night of February 16th, 1804, setting the ship ablaze, and damaging the city's defenses.[98] The forces, by the way, were nicknamed "leathernecks" - referring to the leather they wore around their necks to avoid being beheaded by Muslim forces, which apparently has remained a favorite method of execution among them.

Pope Pius VII, viewing the war as a clash of cultures declared following the raid that America had "done more for the cause of Christianity than the most powerful nations of Christendom have done for ages."[99]

Jefferson then began looking for ways to send two more frigates to the Mediterranean, with a helping hand from Congress that approved a new tax and spending for the war.

The campaign against the Barbary forces continued, finally concluding in June of 1805 with Karamanli signing a

---

[98] London, Joshua. "Victory in Tripoli: Lessons for the War on Terrorism." Heritage Foundation, May 4, 2006.
http://www.heritage.org/defense/report/victory-tripoli-lessons-the-war-terrorism
[99] Of course, as Christopher Hitchens notes, "His Holiness was evidently unaware that the Treaty of Tripoli, which in 1797 had attempted to formalize the dues that America would pay for access to the Mediterranean, stated in its preamble that the United States had no quarrel with the Muslim religion and was in no sense a Christian country. Of course, those secularists like myself who like to cite this treaty must concede that its conciliatory language was part of America's attempt to come to terms with Barbary demands."

peace treaty fearing continued advances from American forces. In the end, 800 soldiers part of the Barbary forces were killed, and 1200 were wounded. Only 35 Americans were killed, and 64 wounded. Jefferson paid a $60,000 ransom for the American prisoners the pirates held - and that was the last time they saw a paycheck from America.

While the motivations for America fighting the war were economic, not religious, there are plenty of lessons to be learned from the First Barbary War (the second lasted only a year - with Barbary forces suffering five times as many casualties as America). Mainly, Muslim aggression was justified solely on the basis of their religion. There's no American imperialism to blame. There's no Islamophobia driving people to extremism. Maybe liberals could blame poverty (another favorite excuse for extremism) - but who the hell wasn't poor in the 1800s?

Our motivations were economic - while theirs were economic and (predominantly) religious. They weren't armed with AK-47s and explosives, but were clearly the Islamic "militants" of their day (with "militants" put in quotation marks only because the pirates understood Islam the same way the rest of the Muslim world did).

We took the justifications of the barbary pirates at face value. Why not take the extremists of today at face value? Until the barbarism of the Koran is actually acknowledged can meaningful steps be taken towards actually reforming the religion, and combating its most extreme fringes.

CHAPTER SIX
Islam and the Left

Progressives are more than happy to deem any criticism of "Islamophobic." I prefer to deem their defense of any wrong in the world connected to Islam (solely because it's connected to Islam) as a form of "Islamophilia."

The polemicist Douglas Murray published a book by that latter name in 2014, in which he defines the term as "the expression of disproportionate adoration of Islam," elaborating "I don't say – because I don't think – that Islam has no redeeming features or that the religion has achieved nothing. But it seems strange to me that so many people today can be quite so asinine and supine when it comes to the religion. No other religion in the world today receives the kind of pass that Islam gets. Most religions currently get a hell of a time. But Islam does not."

After every terror attack we're reminded that most Muslims don't support such acts - as if anyone ever argued that they do. Meanwhile, the same progressives are more than happy to drop the "not all" argument when it comes to any other form of violence that could bolster their cause.

Let's take the far-left Salon.com as an example. Following the Boston Marathon Bombing they ran an article with the headline "Muslims don't need to apologize for the Tsarnaevs." For anyone who doesn't remember, the Tsarnaev brothers were the two responsible for the attacks. And heck - Salon is right in this case. Why should Muslims apologize for something that they didn't do?[100]

---

[100] https://twitter.com/salon/status/326371333762080768?lang=en

But look what happens when something fits their narrative. Want to push a narrative of rampant racism and white supremacy in America? Take an incident like the Dylan Roof massacre at a black church in which nine were killed - and they can run an article headlined "White America must answer for the Charleston church massacre."[101] Or maybe a piece on mass public shootings titled "Why is it always a white guy: The roots of modern, violent rage," in which they try to explain why white people are always the first to violence (even though whites are underrepresented in the U.S. prison system for violent crimes, and Asians are the most overrepresented perpetrator in mass public shootings).[102]

Among the other gems from Salon include:

- "Let's hope the Boston Marathon bomber is a white American"- David Sirota, 4/16/2011[103]
- "Sorry, conservatives, but there is nothing surprising about anti-choice terrorism." - Amanda Marcotte, 11/30/2015[104]
- "10 worst examples of Christian or far-right terrorism." - Alex Henderson 8/3/2013[105]

---

[101] https://twitter.com/salon/status/611803115315154944

[102] Ford, Dana. "Who commits mass shootings?" CNN, July 24, 2015. http://www.cnn.com/2015/06/27/us/mass-shootings.
[103] http://www.salon.com/2013/04/16/lets_hope_the_boston_marathon_bomber_is_a_white_american/
[104] http://www.salon.com/2015/11/30/sorry_conservatives_but_there_is_nothing_surprising_about_anti_choice_terrorism/
[105] http://www.salon.com/2013/08/03/the_10_worst_examples_of_christian_or_far_right_terrorism_partner/

There are countless other examples I could point to in which publications remind us that all Muslims are individuals and not responsible for the actions of those on the fringes - but happy to lump together those they disagree with. I've never seen a liberal make the "not all" argument in defense of gun owners following a mass public shooting, for example.

Above all else, as they try to defend Muslims in the name of tolerance, they're committing the worst form of bigotry: the soft bigotry of low expectations. After a massacre like the one at Charlie Hebdo in France there was no shortage of Islamophiles debating whether or not the attack was "provoked." Meanwhile across the Atlantic, one of the most popular and acclaimed Broadway plays since 2011 has been The Book of Mormon - which lampoons the religion it's titled after.

Were there any concerns of retaliation from Mormons? Did Broadway need enhanced security in case of a potential terror attack? Did the play's writers and actors need to go into hiding following endless death threats? Such a scenario is comical to ponder, and the answer is an obvious "no."

Instead, the Mormon Church responded by taking out advertisements in some of the play's playbills reading "you've seen the play, now read the book" and "the book is always better."

What would you say the odds are that the same would be the case if "The Qur'an" was the next big play on Broadway?

Zero.

What was the difference? The religions, of course. There's a bizarre denial of the fact that all religions are not the same. Claiming that all religions are the same would be like claiming all books or all movies are the same simply because they're in the category of books and movies.

Unfortunately, religious extremism can't be dismissed as a few crazies in every religious group. While one can positively argue that each religion does have its extremists, in no other religion is it as prevalent as in Islam.

Islam and Peace - the Golden Verse

There is no shortage of American politicians offering up their own "evidences" that Islam is a religion of peace - and there's one verse in particular I'd like to examine that the apologists cite. This verse does more to prove how little they understand than I could ever hope to by quoting a random violent verse in the Qur'an.

It's a verse that every apologist for Islam has cited once (though rarely from a Muslim apologist for Islam), including former President Barack Obama. In praising the supposed peaceful teachings contained within the Qur'an, Obama cited verse 5:32. "The Holy Qur'an teaches that whoever kills an innocent, it is as if he killed all mankind; and whoever saves a person, it is as if he has saved all of mankind." The only Muslim I've seen cite the verse was Rep Keith Ellison during an appearance on HBO's Real Time With Bill Maher (against charges that the Qur'an is a "hate filled book").[106] (See: Politically Incorrect Guide to Islam p. 11-13)

---

[106] HBO's Real Time With Bill Maher, aired March 11th, 2011.

I was even more surprised to see German journalist Jurgen Todenhofer cite the verse in his book "My Journey Into the Heart of Terror" - which documents the ten days he spent within ISIS territory (he was given a guarantee of protection from the Caliph Abu Bakr al-Baghdadi). At the end of his book, he pens an open letter to ISIS to try to dissuade them from their ways.[107]

He, without a hint of irony, refers to this verse as one that Baghdadi "apparently is not familiar with,": "And here are the surahs you have sinned against most. The killing of a person... is as great a sin as murdering all of mankind. However, to save a life would be as great a virtue as to save all of mankind. 5:32."

Well, it's doubtful he'll convince ISIS with that logic - because unlike him, ISIS knows their holy book inside and out. Baghdadi in particular, considering he has a Ph.D. in Islamic Studies. Though on the other hand, you don't need a Ph.D. to read the verse that comes directly afterwards, which mandates punishments for those who fight against Allah and Muhammad, including crucifixion and amputation.

Qur'an 5:33 reads "Indeed, the penalty for those who wage war against Allah and His Messenger and strive upon earth [to cause] corruption is none but that they be killed or crucified or that their hands and feet be cut off from opposite sides or that they be exiled from the land. That is for them a disgrace in this world; and for them in the Hereafter is a great punishment."

Great - so one verse prohibiting murder (presumably only against other Muslims)- followed up by mandating

---

[107] Todenhöfer, Jürgen. My Journey into the Heart of Terror: Ten Days in the Islamic State. Vancouver: Greystone, 2016. Page 229.

essentially the torture and murder of those who oppose Islam.

How peaceful.

And speaking of peace, Obama followed up that doozy by citing Qur'an 9:119, stating "as the Holy Qur'an tells us, 'Be conscious of God and speak always the truth.' That is what I try to do - to speak the truth as best I can."

Hilariously, that particular verse is about fighting nonbelievers, and continues "...O ye who believe! Fight those of the disbelievers who are near to you, and let them find harshness in you, and know that Allah is with those who keep their duty."[108]

So the argument that at its core, the Qur'an is actually a peaceful book misinterpreted by extremists is bogus (and of course, we'll examine some of the most satanic verses later in this book), so what other arguments are in the arsenal of the Islamic apologist?

Overview: What Does the Muslim World Believe? The Conflict with Liberalism

Can there even be a "Muslim" position on anything?

A common theme from Islam's apologists (particularly the non-Muslim ones) is to respond to any statement about Muslim beliefs as if they're merely a baseless generalization. The response is phrased along the

---

[108] For a good discussion on the two verses in question, see Spencer, Robert. The Complete Infidel's Guide to the Qur'an. Washington, DC: Regnery Pub., 2009. Pages 11-13.

lines of "that's just what so and so believes, and there are 1.6 billion Muslims in the world, so we can't generalize."

Saudi Arabia's treatment of women? That's only representative of Saudi Arabia - and there are 1.6 billion Muslims in the world! Pakistan executing atheists? Their epidemic of honor killings? Only representative of Pakistan - and there are 1.6 billion Muslims in the world! Women being stoned for adultery in Afghanistan? That's just Afghanistan, and can hardly be used to make a claim about Muslims. There are an entire 1.6 billion of them after all!

But unbeknownst to those making such an argument, generalizing what Muslims believe as doctrine doesn't mean exactly 100% of them believe them. It means that there's unanimous agreement - and those issues that there does tend to be near-unanimous agreement are on are completely antithetical to Western, and liberal values.

Let's take a look at just a few, starting with the law.

Is there a conflict between Western law and Islamic law? Well, that goes without saying (and will be discussed all throughout this book) - but do Muslims really care about it, or are they like the 99% of Catholic women who use birth control despite the Church's opposition?

Not really. The overwhelming majority of Muslims globally both believe Sharia to be the revealed word of God - and that it should take precedence over Western law. Naturally, the more devout a Muslim is, the more likely they are to support implementation of Sharia.

Just look at the following figures, courtesy of research from the Pew Research Center.[109]

Sharia as the Revealed Word of God

% of Muslims who say sharia is ...

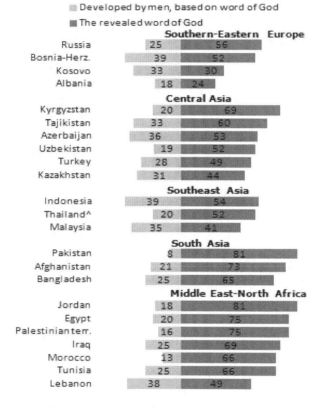

Developed by men, based on word of God
The revealed word of God

Southern-Eastern Europe
	Developed by men	Revealed word
Russia	25	56
Bosnia-Herz.	39	52
Kosovo	33	30
Albania	18	24

Central Asia
Kyrgyzstan	20	69
Tajikistan	33	60
Azerbaijan	36	53
Uzbekistan	19	52
Turkey	28	49
Kazakhstan	31	44

Southeast Asia
Indonesia	39	54
Thailand^	20	52
Malaysia	35	41

South Asia
Pakistan	8	81
Afghanistan	21	73
Bangladesh	25	65

Middle East-North Africa
Jordan	18	81
Egypt	20	75
Palestinian terr.	16	75
Iraq	25	69
Morocco	13	66
Tunisia	25	66
Lebanon	38	49

^Interviews conducted with Muslims in five southern provinces only.

PEW RESEARCH CENTER Q66.

[109] "Chapter 1: Beliefs About Sharia." Pew Research Center, April 30, 2013. http://www.pewforum.org/2013/04/30/the-worlds-muslims-religion-politics-society-beliefs-about-sharia/

Favor or Oppose Making Sharia the Law of the Land?

% of Muslims who favor making Islamic law the official law in their country

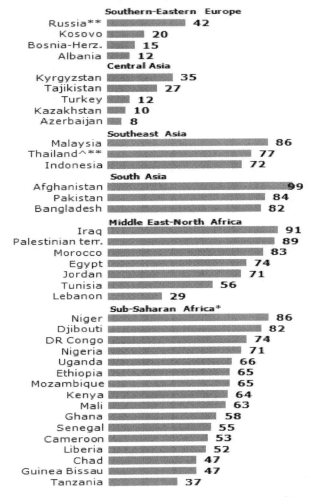

Southern-Eastern Europe
- Russia** 42
- Kosovo 20
- Bosnia-Herz. 15
- Albania 12

Central Asia
- Kyrgyzstan 35
- Tajikistan 27
- Turkey 12
- Kazakhstan 10
- Azerbaijan 8

Southeast Asia
- Malaysia 86
- Thailand^** 77
- Indonesia 72

South Asia
- Afghanistan 99
- Pakistan 84
- Bangladesh 82

Middle East-North Africa
- Iraq 91
- Palestinian terr. 89
- Morocco 83
- Egypt 74
- Jordan 71
- Tunisia 56
- Lebanon 29

Sub-Saharan Africa*
- Niger 86
- Djibouti 82
- DR Congo 74
- Nigeria 71
- Uganda 66
- Ethiopia 65
- Mozambique 65
- Kenya 64
- Mali 63
- Ghana 58
- Senegal 55
- Cameroon 53
- Liberia 52
- Chad 47
- Guinea Bissau 47
- Tanzania 37

*Data for all countries except Niger from "Tolerance and Tension: Islam and Christianity in Sub-Saharan Africa."
^Interviews conducted with Muslims in five southern provinces only.
**Question was modified to ask if sharia should be the law of the land in Muslim areas.

PEW RESEARCH CENTER Q79a.

Muslims Who Pray More Frequently Are More Likely to Favor Sharia as Law of the Land

% of Muslims who favor implementing Islamic law as the law of the land

	Pray several times a day	Pray less often	Diff.
Russia*	65	28	+37
Lebanon	39	11	+28
Palestinian terr.	95	68	+27
Tunisia	64	39	+25
Kyrgyzstan	54	30	+24
Bosnia-Herz.	29	12	+17
Malaysia	90	74	+16
Morocco	88	73	+15
Indonesia	74	64	+10
Turkey	18	8	+10
Bangladesh	88	79	+9
Kosovo	25	16	+9

*Question was modified to ask if sharia should be the law of the land in Muslim areas.
Only countries where differences are statistically significant are shown.

PEW RESEARCH CENTER Q61 and Q79a.

But wait, you might say, Sharia law doesn't mean what you think. Sure there are the harsh parts that we all know (chopping the hands off thieves, stoning adulterers, executing apostates), but that's a small fraction of what Sharia Law commands. According to Yassmin Abdel-Magied, who thinks that Islam is the "most feminist religion" (yes, really), "me praying five times a day is Sharia law."[110]

---

[110] Jacqui Lambie and Yassmin Abdel-Magied on "Q&A," 13 February 2017.

She is correct. Among the Sharia, we can find plenty of rules that aren't completely barbaric - but so what? Would someone defend the Nazis by arguing that gassing Jews was only a small percentage of all they did? Of course not. And unlike Abdel-Magied, most Muslims don't pick and choose what divine laws to follow.

Just look at the following polling (again from Pew),[111] showing an overwhelming support among Muslims for chopping the hands off of thieves, stoning adulterers, honor killings, death to apostates, and disdain for homosexuals.

---

[111] Ibid.

Do You Favor Corporal Punishments for Crimes Such as Theft?

Among Muslims who say sharia should be the law of the land, % who favor corporal punishment

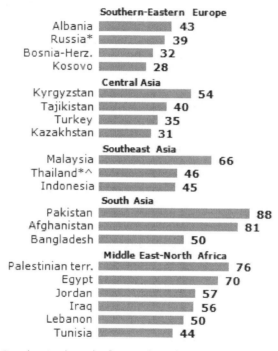

Southern-Eastern Europe
Albania	43
Russia*	39
Bosnia-Herz.	32
Kosovo	28

Central Asia
Kyrgyzstan	54
Tajikistan	40
Turkey	35
Kazakhstan	31

Southeast Asia
Malaysia	66
Thailand*^	46
Indonesia	45

South Asia
Pakistan	88
Afghanistan	81
Bangladesh	50

Middle East-North Africa
Palestinian terr.	76
Egypt	70
Jordan	57
Iraq	56
Lebanon	50
Tunisia	44

Based on Muslims who favor making sharia the law of the land.
*Based on Muslims who favor making sharia the law in Muslim areas.
^Interviews conducted with Muslims in five southern provinces only.
Results for Azerbaijan not shown due to small sample size.

PEW RESEARCH CENTER Q79a and Q92c.

Stoning as Punishment for Adultery

Among Muslims who say sharia should be the law of the land, % who favor stoning as a punishment for adultery

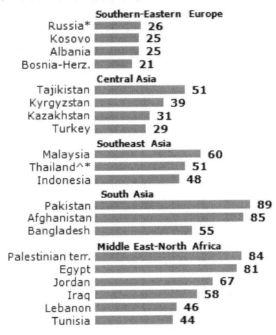

Southern-Eastern Europe
Russia* — 26
Kosovo — 25
Albania — 25
Bosnia-Herz. — 21

Central Asia
Tajikistan — 51
Kyrgyzstan — 39
Kazakhstan — 31
Turkey — 29

Southeast Asia
Malaysia — 60
Thailand^* — 51
Indonesia — 48

South Asia
Pakistan — 89
Afghanistan — 85
Bangladesh — 55

Middle East-North Africa
Palestinian terr. — 84
Egypt — 81
Jordan — 67
Iraq — 58
Lebanon — 46
Tunisia — 44

Based on Muslims who favor making sharia the law of the land.
*Based on Muslims who favor making sharia the law in Muslim areas.
^Interviews conducted with Muslims in five southern provinces only.
Results for Azerbaijan not shown due to small sample size.

PEW RESEARCH CENTER Q79a and Q92d.

126

Is Homosexual Behavior Moral?

% of Muslims who say it is ...

▓ Morally wrong   ■ Morally acceptable

Southern-Eastern Europe

Country	Morally wrong	Morally acceptable
Albania	83	5
Bosnia-Herz.	83	5
Kosovo	73	3
Russia	89	1

Central Asia

Country	Morally wrong	Morally acceptable
Kyrgyzstan	76	3
Turkey	85	3
Kazakhstan	92	1
Azerbaijan	92	0
Tajikistan	82	0

Southeast Asia

Country	Morally wrong	Morally acceptable
Malaysia	94	2
Indonesia	95	1
Thailand^	99	1

South Asia

Country	Morally wrong	Morally acceptable
Bangladesh	67	10
Pakistan	90	1

Middle East-North Africa

Country	Morally wrong	Morally acceptable
Tunisia	91	2
Jordan	96	2
Iraq	77	1
Palestinian terr.	89	1
Egypt	94	1
Lebanon	97	1

Sub-Saharan Africa*

Country	Morally wrong	Morally acceptable
Uganda	77	12
Mozambique	79	11
Guinea Bissau	71	6
Djibouti	80	6
Liberia	90	6
DR Congo	87	3
Chad	92	2
Kenya	96	2
Niger	90	1
Senegal	90	1
Mali	91	1
Tanzania	91	1
Nigeria	94	1
Ghana	97	1
Ethiopia	98	0
Cameroon	99	0

*Data for all countries except Niger from "Tolerance and Tension: Islam and Christianity in Sub-Saharan Africa."
^Interviews conducted with Muslims in five southern provinces only.

PEW RESEARCH CENTER Q84j.

I'll elaborate more on the response to the question of homosexuality, because the question Pew asked merely had to do with whether or not they think homosexuality is moral.

Certainly many Christians in America would also agree with such a statement - but their opposition would amount to nothing more than opposing same sex marriage. Heck, given the individualist nature of American values, even many of those who find it immoral don't care about gay marriage because it doesn't affect them, or at the very least support civil unions.

That isn't the same in the Muslim world. Let's just take a look at the countries where homosexuality is punished by death - and see if you can notice what they all have in common: Afghanistan, Iran, Saudi Arabia, Yemen, Somalia, Sudan, Nigeria, Mauritania, the United Arab Emirates (disputed)[112] and Qatar. The only country on the list where the population isn't overwhelmingly Muslim (90%+) is Nigeria, which is still a Muslim majority nation nonetheless (50% Muslim, 40% Christian).[113]

And those are just the countries where homosexuality is punishable by death! The same pattern emerges in the countries where homosexuality is illegal - but gays at least don't get killed for it. Algeria, Morocco, Libya, South Sudan, Uzbekistan, Malaysia - the list goes on, and

---

[112] According to the Washington Post, lawyers in the UAE disagree on whether federal law commands the death penalty for consensual homosexual acts, or only for homosexual rape.

[113] Bearak, Max and Darla Cameron. "Here are the 10 countries where homosexuality may be punished by death." Washington Post, June 16, 2016. https://www.washingtonpost.com/news/worldviews/wp/2016/06/13/here-are-the-10-countries-where-homosexuality-may-be-punished-by-death-2

you know what the dominant religion in those counties is. India is the only non-Muslim country I spotted on the list.

Anyway, back to more polls:

Support for Sharia and Views on Honor Killings

Among Muslims who ...

	Favor sharia	Oppose sharia	Diff.
% who say *never* justified when female stands accused			
Albania	34	74	-40
Tunisia	44	74	-30
Tajikistan	33	61	-28
Kazakhstan	63	89	-26
Lebanon	31	53	-22
Bosnia-Herz.	64	82	-18
Kosovo	48	63	-15
Kyrgyzstan	52	66	-14
Russia	53	66	-13
% who say *never* justified when male stands accused			
Albania	31	75	-44
Lebanon	38	63	-25
Tajikistan	36	59	-23
Tunisia	53	73	-20
Russia	57	77	-20
Kazakhstan	69	88	-19
Kosovo	46	63	-17
Bosnia-Herz.	65	81	-16
Kyrgyzstan	49	64	-15

Only countries where differences are statistically significant are shown.

PEW RESEARCH CENTER Q79a, Q53 and Q54.

Source: Pew Research Center[114]

---

[114] "The World's Muslims: Chapter 3: Morality." Pew Research Center, April 30th, 2013. http://www.pewforum.org/2013/04/30/the-worlds-muslims-religion-politics-society-morality/

Death Penalty for Leaving Islam

Among Muslims who say sharia should be the law of the land, % who favor the death penalty for converts

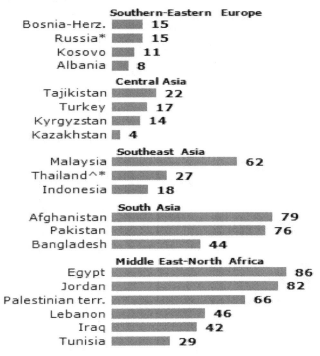

Southern-Eastern Europe
- Bosnia-Herz. — 15
- Russia* — 15
- Kosovo — 11
- Albania — 8

Central Asia
- Tajikistan — 22
- Turkey — 17
- Kyrgyzstan — 14
- Kazakhstan — 4

Southeast Asia
- Malaysia — 62
- Thailand^* — 27
- Indonesia — 18

South Asia
- Afghanistan — 79
- Pakistan — 76
- Bangladesh — 44

Middle East-North Africa
- Egypt — 86
- Jordan — 82
- Palestinian terr. — 66
- Lebanon — 46
- Iraq — 42
- Tunisia — 29

Based on Muslims who favor making sharia the law of the land.
*Based on Muslims who favor making sharia the law in Muslim areas.
^Interviews conducted with Muslims in five southern provinces only.
Results for Azerbaijan not shown due to small sample size.

PEW RESEARCH CENTER Q79a and Q92b.

Source: Pew Research Center[115]

[115] "The World's Muslims: Chapter 1: Beliefs About Sharia." Pew Research Center.

Granted, in some cases we "only" average fifteen of so percent of the nation believing that ex-Muslims should be killed, or "only" see 25 percent supporting stoning for adultery. Even while that shows there isn't unanimous agreement in those countries on such barbarism, it's still shocking. In absence of Islam, the numbers would undoubtedly be closer to zero (for the latter question polled).

Indeed, this turns the "but there are 1.6 billion Muslims" argument on its head. Even if we were to suppose that every nation's Muslims were as "moderate" as those in Albania on the issue of death for apostates (8 percent support), that's 128 million Muslims with such a belief. If your apostasy is made public, only one in 128 million needs to act on it.

And of course, the agreement on these issues, on average, is overwhelmingly higher.

CHAPTER SEVEN
Apologists & Arguments: Islam's Apologists in America

Linda Sarsour

Only in the world of identity politics can someone with views that are objectively regressive be a hero among progressives. Enter: Linda Sarsour.

Sarsour has been active in the Muslim-American community in New York for the majority of her adult life. In 2011 she became the executive director of the Arab American Association of New York after holding a handful of other positions in the organization.

She never fails to mention her broad portfolio of identities whenever she's interviewed. She's not just Linda Sarsour - she's a Palestinian, Muslim-American, from Brooklyn New York who wears a hijab. She was an Obama White House "Champion of Change," spoke at the 15th annual convention of the Muslim American Society and Islamic Circle of North America (among countless other public appearances), and has close ties to our friends at CAIR, who will be discussed shortly.

Her activism was mainly confined to New York prior to the election of Donald Trump, in which she rose to national prominence for her role in the "Women's March" that took place the day after the inauguration. The other notable organizers included Tamika Mallory, Carmen Perez, and Bob Bland.

By and large, the March was a success. The rally attracted 400,000 women to Washington D.C. according to some estimates, and there wasn't a single arrest - so no problem there.

It was extremely ironic however that Sarsour was the organizer of a march that claimed to be for women's rights (and let's be honest, it was really just an anti-Trump march under another name), given her own religious stances that completely betray any concept of women's rights.

Be careful before you criticize those at the march for focusing on leftist nonsense over issues actually affecting women (such as their treatment under Islam in the Middle East) – because you'll quickly be informed by Sarsour that there's no problem to be seen there.

Here are just a handful of their tweets that were dug up after she rose to notoriety:[116]

> 11/16/14 - 10 weeks of PAID maternity leave in Saudi Arabia. Yes PAID. And ur worrying about women driving. Puts us to shame.
> 1/29/15 - FYI - mandated head covering for Muslim women in Saudi Arabia is the LEAST of their worries. Stop making it THE ISSUES. It's not.
> 1/29/15 - There are Muslim countries who have women presidents for God's sake. In Saudi Arabia - ur boogeyman Islamic state, women r in parliament.
> 5/12/15 - You'll know you're living under Sharia Law if suddenly all your loans & credit cards become interest free. Sounds nice, doesn't it?

---

[116] These tweets were quickly deleted by Sarsour after they came to light. You can find an archive at:
https://thesecularbrownie.com/2017/01/24/linda-sarsours-awkward-defensiveness-over-saudi-oppression-that-the-left-seems-to-ignore/

And did I mention she's gone on MSNBC before to complain that States passing anti-Sharia bills interferes with Muslims practicing their faith?[117]

So to recap logic according to Linda Sarsour:

- Forcing women to cover themselves head-to-toe in black polyester in the Middle East is the last thing they worry about.

- Not giving women a particular government handout is oppressive while preventing them from driving is not.

- You can judge the status of women in a nation with over 15 million of them by the fact that a few are allowed in parliament. We just need to ignore the fact that women weren't allowed in parliament until 2013 and pretend that it's always been this way.[118] Additionally, are we supposed to presume that these women are being driven by their fathers to work?

- Implementing a legal system that cuts the hands of thieves, stones women as a punishment for being raped, and commands homosexuals to be thrown off buildings is the reasonable tradeoff for not having to pay interest on loans and credit cards. Good luck

[117] Laila, Cristina. "Flashback-Organizer Of Women's March, Linda Sarsour To Rachel Maddow: 'Muslim Children Are Executed In The U.S.'" The Gateway Pundit, http://www.thegatewaypundit.com/2017/01/flashback-organizer-womens-march-linda-sarsour-rachel-maddow-muslim-children-executed-u-s-video/
[118] "Breakthrough in Saudi Arabia: women allowed in parliament." Al-Arabiya News, January 11, 2013. http://www.alarabiya.net/articles/2013/01/11/259881.html

getting a loan in the first place under those conditions (Hint: you won't, which is why in Islamic finance there's a whole list of mental gymnastics one goes through so they technically aren't being charged "interest" on their loans - but it's just a rose by another name).

A number of women at the march could be seen with signs stating that they wouldn't go back to the 1950s when it comes to women's rights. Sarsour would rather they go back to how they were in the 1500s.

Even if we're to excuse her religiously inspired insanity, they're hardly her only "questionable comments." In fact one comment in particular, if it were uttered by Donald Trump, would see those at the women's march calling for impeachment.

Back in 2013, she tweeted about women's rights activists Brigitte Gabriel and Ayaan Hirsi Ali "Brigitte Gabriel = Ayaan Hirsi Ali. She's asking 4 an a$$ whippin. I wish I could take their vaginas away - they don't deserve to be women."

In the case of Hirsi Ali, someone already tried that. She had suffered genital mutilation as a five-year-old in Somalia, and later fled to the Netherlands to escape an arranged marriage. She made a short film criticizing the treatment of women in Islamic society in 2004 with writer Theo van Gogh — a man later murdered by Islamists in broad daylight. Ali now runs the world's leading organization aimed at ending honor killings and other gender-based violence.[119]

---

[119] The AHA Foundation. See: http://www.theahafoundation.org/

Gabriel, meanwhile, had her home destroyed by Islamic militants during the Lebanese Civil War. She was injured by shrapnel in the attack.

Both women have been exposed to tragedies far removed from the conflictless existence led by Sarsour from her apartment in Brooklyn. Sarsour is lucky in the sense that the only oppression she faces is in her own head.

We all know that if liberals didn't have double standards, they wouldn't have any at all — but who thought a key organizer in a women's march would be this anti-woman?

The continued support for Sarsour despite her views that completely betray the Left's own ideals is a constant reminder that when it comes to insane world of identity politics, the color of a person's skin is much more important than the content of their character.

Sarsour doesn't mean "cockroach" in Arabic for nothing.

A Day Without Women

As if the Women's March organizers didn't milk all the publicity they could, it wasn't long before the band got back together.

Immigrants opposed to Donald Trump's agenda staged a "day without immigrants" on February 16th, 2017, in which legal and illegal immigrants protested by removing themselves from the workforce to show just how needed they are. The legal immigrants apparently didn't get the memo that it's the *illegal* immigrants Trump is opposed to. You'd think the fact that two thirds of the man's wives are immigrants would be a hint.

In the end, it was mostly those in the foodservice industry affected (though a number of schools reported having immigrant students stay home that day). Most immigrants continued to prove their strong work ethic by actually showing up for work despite the protest - and over 100 protesters nationwide were fired for skipping out on work.

Oops.

Determined to exacerbate the wage gap even further (and maybe even get a few women fired while they're at it), the Women's March organizers decided to have a similar event of their own: the Day Without Women.

"On International Women's Day, March 8th, women and our allies will act together for equity, justice, and the human rights of women and all gender-oppressed people, through a one-day demonstration of economic solidarity" read the Women's March's website in advertising the new event.

Women nationwide were encouraged to participate in one (or all) of the following ways:

1. Women take the day off, from paid and unpaid labor. Among the forms of unpaid labor women were to avoid includes "emotional labor." An example of "emotional labor" would be a waitress acting friendly and outgoing at her job - which is apparently a new form of oppression women aren't properly compensated for (trust me - I went uncompensated for my "emotional labor" during my five years in the food service industry, I just didn't call it emotional labor, I called it work).

2. Avoid shopping for one day (with exceptions for small, women- and minority-owned businesses).
3. Wear RED in solidarity with A Day Without A Woman

And for this new event, Sarsour and company moved away from sympathizing with Islamists to enlisting their aid.

According to the New York Post:

> In a manifesto published in The Guardian on Feb. 6, the brains behind the movement are calling for a "new wave of militant feminist struggle."[120]

That's right: militant, not peaceful. And one of the woman behind the document are militant in more than name only.

> The document was co-authored by, among others, Rasmea Yousef Odeh, a convicted terrorist. Odeh, a Palestinian, was convicted in Israel in 1970 for her part in two terrorist bombings, one of which killed two students while they were shopping for groceries. She spent 10 years in prison for her crimes. She then managed to become a US citizen in 2004 by lying about her past (great detective work, INS: Next time, use Google) but was subsequently convicted, in 2014, of immigration fraud for the falsehoods. However, she won the right to a new trial (set for this spring) by claiming she had been suffering from PTSD at the time she lied on her application. Oh, and

---

[120] The relevent Guardian piece can be read at:
https://www.theguardian.com/commentisfree/2017/feb/06/women-strike-trump-resistance-power

in her time as a citizen, she worked for a while as an Obamacare navigator.[121]

According to The Guardian piece, women should spend their day "blocking roads, bridges, and squares, abstaining from domestic, care and sex work" and "boycotting" pro-Trump businesses.

I imagine they only decided to block off traffic upon realizing that men would be having the easiest commutes of their lives in their absence.

Odeh was at least brought to justice (to some extent) following the whole debacle, and agreed to leave the US in exchange for not facing jail time.[122]

A day without women lead to a lifetime without a terrorist.

You go girls.

Reza Aslan

Reza Aslan has made a career for himself as the media's go-to moderate Muslim on demand they can bring on air anytime Islam is in need of a defense. He's extremely happy to flaunt his credentials, claiming to have four degrees in the study of religion, one of which being a Ph.D. in the history of religions, or sociology of religions, depending on

---

[121] Smith, Kyle. "Meet the Terrorist Behind the Next Woman's March." New York Post, February 25, 2017. http://nypost.com/2017/02/25/the-next-womens-march-is-co-organized-by-a-terrorist/?_ga=1.32783866.57636498.1467003386
[122] Richardson, Valerie. "Plea Deal: Rasmea Odeh, convicted terrorist, agrees to leave U.S. in exchange for no jail time." The Washington Times, March 24, 2017. http://www.washingtontimes.com/news/2017/mar/24/rasmea-odeh-convicted-terrorist-agrees-leave-us-ex/

the interview. In reality, one of his two Masters' degrees is a Master of Fine Arts in Fiction Writing (which has clearly come in handy throughout his career), and his Ph.D. is in Sociology. His alma-mater doesn't even offer a Ph.D. in the sociology, or history of religions.

His only full time teaching position has been in creative writing.

Despite his inflated credentials, and the fact that Aslan has never contributed to a single peer reviewed article, he's still heralded as an expert (probably because the actual Qur'anic experts wouldn't tell liberals what they want to hear).

As for his most ridiculous claims, let's get started.

Islam and FGM

Following a notable debate on Real Time With Bill Maher involving Ben Affleck against Sam Harris and Maher, Aslan was invited on CNN to give his take.[123]

According to Aslan, female genital mutilation lacks any connection with Islam. In this particular interview, he made the claim that rather than being an Islamic problem, FGM is a central-African problem. He cited a Unicef study to prove as much, showing that countries with a high prevalence of FGM do tend to be located in central Africa, though there are exceptions in Northern Africa (like Egypt), and the Middle East.

---

[123] All comments were made on "CNN Tonight" on September 29th, 2014.

Now, do I really need to tell you what the religion most prominent in central-Africa is? Just look at the nations where more than eighty percent of women undergo the barbaric procedure: Mali (89%), Guinea (96%), Sierra Leone (88%), Egypt (91%), Sudan (88%), Somalia (96%), Djibouti (93%), and Eritrea (89%).[124]

Now, let's take a look at the religious makeup of those countries (with all data taken from the CIA's World Factbook).

Mali (94.8% Muslim), Guinea (86.7% Muslim), Sierra Leone (60% Muslim - though Pew Research claims 78% Muslim), Egypt (97.2% Muslim), Sudan (97% Muslim), Somalia (99.8% Muslim), Djibouti (94% Muslim), and Eritrea (50% Muslim).

The Unicef study also was kind enough to include quotes from women living in those countries who referred to FGM as a "religious duty."[125] It has nothing to do with central-African culture.

Who knew that a religious expert like Aslan would be so clueless as to the religious composition of Africa? Regardless, contrary to Aslan's claims, there is FGM outside of Africa (even if Unicef didn't include most cases in their study), and in every single case it's in a Muslim majority nation.

As the liberal pundit David Pakman compiled, there's a long list of countries with a significant FGM

---

[124] "Female Genital Mutilation/Cutting: A Statistical Overview and Exploration of the Dynamics of Change." Unicef, July 2013.
https://www.unicef.org/media/files/UNICEF_FGM_report_July_2013_Hi_res.pdf
[125] See page 70 of the report.

problem outside of Africa: Afghanistan, Pakistan, Tajikistan, Bahrain, Iran, Jordan, Palestine, Qatar, Syria, Kurdish Turkey, Oman, United Arab Emirates, Kuwait, Iraqi Kurdistan, Saudi Arabia, Brunei, Indonesia, Maldives, Malaysia, and Indonesia.[126]

There are five countries that are not majority Muslim that experience significant FGM problems - India, Sri Lanka, Singapore, Thailand, and the Philippines - but FGM is practiced exclusively by their Muslim populations.

As Pakman notes, the reason Unicef likely looked only at African nations in their study is simply because it's easier to get reliable data on the matter than in the Middle East. And for that reason, the FGM problem in the Middle East is likely understated.

It's a Central-African problem, an Asian problem, a Middle Eastern problem - but the thread that binds them together is Islam.

One might say it's an Islamic problem.

Islam and Women's Rights

In the same CNN appearance Reza made the FGM flub in, host Don Lemon got on the subject of the treatment of women in Muslim countries, stating "for the most part it is not a free and open society for women in those [Muslim] nations."

Aslan concurred that it certainly isn't in Muslim countries like Iran and Saudi Arabia, but pointed to

---

[126] "Reza Aslan Cannot be Trusted." The David Pakman Show. January 11, 2016. https://www.youtube.com/watch?v=E9RmAo6XVAA

Indonesia, Malaysia, and Bangladesh as examples of Muslim countries where women are free.

In examining that claim, we'll skip over the 93% of Muslim females in Indonesia that are victims of FGM, and that an identical percentage in Malaysia suffer the procedure, which would be ironic (given the claims Aslan made directly prior) if it wasn't so tragic.

According to the United Nations Development Programme "Gender Inequality Index," of 188 countries ranked (1 being the best, 188 being the worst), Indonesia came in 113rd, Malaysia 59th, and Bangladesh 139th. Congratulations to Malaysia for ranking 10 spots above Iran I suppose.

But those rankings are just numbers to you - let's look at some policies in those nations, courtesy of ex-Muslims Muhammad Syed and Sarah Haider.[127]

- In Indonesia, Sharia courts were initially sold as being "optional" - but now enjoy equal status with secular courts when it comes to family matters. The conservative Aceh province even legislates criminal matters via Sharia courts, and nationwide, women who wish to join their armed forces (or become a police officer) have to undergo a virginity test. Needless to say, the motivation for such a test is religious.

- Malaysia has a dual-system of law mandating sharia for Muslims. In accordance with Sharia,

[127] Syed, Muhammad, and Sarah Haider. "Reza Aslan is Wrong About Islam and This is Why." Friendly Atheist, October 5, 2014. http://www.patheos.com/blogs/friendlyatheist/2014/10/05/reza-aslan-is-wrong-about-islam-and-this-is-why/

men can have multiple wives, and discriminate against them in matters related to inheritance. Wives are also prohibited from disobeying "lawful orders" from their husbands.

- An article in Bangladesh's relatively progressive constitution states that "women shall have equal rights with men in all spheres of the state and of the public life" but in the realm of private affairs (marriage, divorce, inheritance, and child custody), "it acknowledges Islam as the state religion and effectively enshrines the application of Islamic law in family affairs. The Constitution thus does nothing to enforce equality in private life."

But back to the gender inequality index. For some context, Saudi Arabia ranked 38th. In other words, every single nation he cited as one where women enjoy rights was ranked worse than the two he acknowledged were detrimental to women's rights (with the exception of Malaysia, which was slightly better than Iran).[128]

Islam and Slavery

"The very first thing that Muhammad did was outlaw slavery" Aslan tells us.

Contain your laughter, and we'll dive straight into this one.

---

[128] "Table Five: Gender Inequality Index." United Nations Development Programme: Human Development Reports. http://hdr.undp.org/en/composite/GII

We'll ignore the sex slaves Mohammad had (given to him by Allah, of course), or the fact that Mohammad himself bought slaves - all of which is documented in the Qur'an and hadiths (Qur'an 33:50 and Sahih Muslim 3901, respectively). Let's look at how the heck Aslan arrived at this conclusion, and why he thinks this is thanks to Islam given that the Qur'an makes no comments condemning slavery.

Like many of his statement, it's "technically" true. Mohammad banned slavery among Muslims - nothing more, nothing less.

When Sam Harris pointed this out to Aslan on Twitter, Reza replied in flaunting his credentials for the millionth time, writing "Hey Sam. I'm thinking of writing a book on neuroscience. I don't need to actually research. I'll just do what you do." [129]

Ironically, it's Aslan who needs to do more research, and it's in the field he claims to be an expert in. Had he done that, he would've learned that Mohammad's prohibition of Muslim slavery caused the slave trade to expand outward to abide by Islam's rules.

Historian Bernard Lewis calls it one of the "sad paradoxes of human history," that "humanitarian reforms brought by Islam resulted in a vast development of the slave trade inside, and still more outside, the Islamic empire." He continues, noting that the prohibition of enslaving other Muslims led to the mass importation of non-Muslim slaves.[130]

---

[129] https://twitter.com/rezaaslan/status/631898636171931648
[130] Lewis, Bernard. Race and Slavery in the Middle East: An Historical Enquiry. New York: Oxford UP, 1992. Page 10.

Personally, I dispute that there's anything paradoxical here. One humanitarian act (outlawing slavery among those who buy what Mohammad's selling) doesn't negate the authorization to take non-Muslim slaves and sex slaves. In fact, it's more of a selling point for the religion if anything. Enslave others, and be protected from slavery yourself.

Lastly, Saudi Arabia, the country in which the religion of Islam originated (in the cities of Mecca and Medina), didn't outlaw slavery until 1962 (thanks to American pressure, by the way). There were 300,000 people enslaved at the time[131] (out of a total population of 4,346,000 - so 7% of the total population was enslaved).

CAIR

Following any terrorist attack, you'll find the Council on American Islamic Relations on the scene to serve as PR for the Muslim community, while acting under the facade of being a civil rights organization.

Incredibly, for a group that constantly reminds us that all Muslims are not terrorists (which they're obviously right about), their origins indicate that they wouldn't mind if they were.

Due to their origins, foreign governments are willing to do what ours won't: designate them as a terrorist organization, which the United Arab Emirates did in 2014. CAIR responded in a statement: "We call on the United Arab Emirates cabinet to review this list and remove organizations

[131] Lord, Christopher. "Falling Out of Love With Saudi Arabia." East West, May 27, 2016. http://eastwest.eu/en/opinioni/open-doors/falling-out-of-love-with-saudi-arabia

146

such as CAIR, the Muslim American Society (MAS) and other civil society organizations that peacefully promote civil and democratic rights and that oppose terrorism whenever it occurs, wherever it occurs and whoever carries it out." They also described the decision as a "bizarre" move.

The UAE was having none of their excuses. "We cannot accept incitement or [terror] funding when we look at some of these organizations. For many countries, the definition of terror is that you have to carry a weapon and terrorize people. For us, it's far beyond that. We cannot tolerate even the smallest and tiniest amount of terrorism," stated UAE Foreign Affairs Minister Sheikh Abdullah bin Zayed Al-Nahyan in response.[132] The main justification for the designation comes from controversy CAIR was the center of in 2007, when they were named along with 300 other unindicted co-conspirators in a case regarding funding to extremist groups, including Hamas and the Muslim Brotherhood. It also doesn't help CAIR's cause that they were funded, in part, by money from Hamas.[133]

Well, I'm sure those in the UAE are just a bunch of Islamophobes.

Most Muslims aren't terrorists - but if they're employed by CAIR, there's a higher chance that they are. At least seven CAIR board members or staff members have

---

[132] Qazvini, Michael. "Here Are 5 Things You Need to Know About the Council on American Islamic Relations." The Daily Wire, December 4th, 2015. http://www.dailywire.com/news/1592/here-are-5-things-you-need-know-about-council-michael-qazvini
[133] Emerson, Steven. "Funding Ties With HLF and Foreign Donors Show CAIR's True Agenda." The Investigative Project on Terrorism. March 25, 2008. https://www.investigativeproject.org/622/funding-ties-with-hlf-and-foreign-donors-show-cairs-agenda

been denied entry to the US, were indicted on or pled guilty to terror charges.

Those individuals are Siraj Wahhaj, Bassem Khafagi, Randall ("Ismail") Royer, Ghassan Elashi, Rabih Haddad, Muthanna Al-Hanooti, and Nabil Sadoun. Let's go through the list.

Siraj Wahhaj - According to the website of CAIR Minnesota, "Siraj Wahhaj is one of the most admired Muslim leaders and speakers in America. He is the imam of Al-Taqwa Mosque in Brooklyn, NY and serves on the executive committee of the Muslim Alliance in North America (MANA). He previously served on the national board of the Council on American-Islamic Relations."[134]

They also note that in 1991, Wahhaj made history as the first Muslim to offer the opening prayer at the U.S. House of Representatives. They don't mention that a mere four years later, he was among the 170 people identified as unindicted co-conspirators in the 1993 World Trade Center bombing.

Despite never being charged, he did defend the convicted bomb plotters, and called the FBI and CIA the "real terrorists."

But let's get back to 1991. That was also the year that he preached that "Wherever you came from, you came to America. And you came for one reason and one reason only - to establish Allah's deen." And what does that entail? The creation of an Islamic State, of course. "There will never be an Islamic State, never, until there's first an Islamic State of

---

[134] "Imam Siraj Wahhaj." CAIR Minnesota, last updated May 7, 2015. http://cairmn.com/2-uncategorised/313-imam-siraj-wahhaj.html

mind" he said, continuing that one shouldn't get involved in politics because it's "the American thing to do," but rather that "you get involved in politics because politics are a weapon to use in the cause of Islam."[135]

Would you also believe that he supports the implementation of Sharia Law over democracy? That should go without saying. According to him, "If Allah says 100 strikes, 100 strikes it is. If Allah says cut off their hand, you cut off their hand. If Allah says stone them to death, through the Prophet Muhammad, then you stone them to death, because it's the obedience of Allah and his messenger— nothing personal."

Well thank God it's not personal.

Bassem Khafagi - Khafagi is the former community relations director of CAIR. That was until he was sentenced in September 2003 to 10 months in prison after being charged with funneling money to promote terrorism through the Islamic Assembly of North America.

Afterwards he was deported to Egypt, where he eventually became a presidential candidate. On March 12, 2012, he said on Egyptian television, "as a Muslim Egyptian, I am convinced of [the need to] complete the implementation of Islamic law in Egypt. I do not hide this truth in any way, because it is in keeping with the inclination of the Egyptian people." He added, "As president, I will personally assist in

---

[135] Siraj Wahhaj, "The Muslim Agenda in the New World Order," Islamic Association of Northern Texas, Dallas, Texas, November 15, 1991.

the completion of the correct implementation of the shari'a, by consulting the experts [in Islamic law]."[136]

Randall ("Ismail") Roger - Roger worked for CAIR as a communications specialist in 1997, and worked there through at least October 2001. That means he worked for CAIR for at least a month after he was stopped for a traffic violation by police in September of 2001 - and was found with an AK-47 style rifle with 219 rounds of ammunition on him.

Now I'm as pro-gun as anyone else, but it was what he was planning on using it for that's the problem.

In June 2003, Royer was indicted with ten others for committing jihad in Kashmir. He was charged with spreading propaganda for the terrorist organization Lashkar-e-Taiba, and for firing at Indian positions in Kashmir.[137]

CAIR attempted to distance themselves from him, noting that he was also a former employee of Starbucks (and we wouldn't try to link Starbucks to terrorism, would we?). That was really the best argument they had.

Still, it's refreshing that they at least acknowledged a terrorist among their ranks this time.

---

[136] "Bassem Khafagi, Former Community Relations Director of Council on American-Islamic Relations (CAIR) and A Founder of Islamic Assembly of North America (IANA) - Who In 2003 Was Convicted In U.S. and Deported - Says In His Presidential Campaign in Egypt: I Pledge To 'Complete Implementation of Islamic Law." The Middle East Media Research Institute, March 14, 2012. https://www.memri.org/reports/bassem-khafagi-former-community-relations-director-council-american-islamic-relations-cair
[137] "The Suspect Ties of CAIR Officials, Fundraisers, & Trainers." The Investigative Project on Terrorism. http://www.investigativeproject.org/documents/misc/111.pdf

Ghassan Elashi - Elashi was a founding member of both the Holy Land Foundation for Relief and Development and the founding of a CAIR chapter in Texas.

Unlike the others, he's been charged multiple times. Quoting from Discover the Networks:

In December 2002, Elashi was arrested for conspiracy, money laundering, and dealing in the property of a designated terrorist. According to prosecutors, he and his two brothers (Bayan and Basman) had tried to hide Hamas official Mousa Mohammed Abu Marzook's $250,000 investment in Elashi's Texas-based computer company (Infocom), and then had funneled payments to Marzook in return.

In April 2005 Elashi was convicted on all 21 federal counts against him. He was sentenced to 80 months in prison.

On July 23, 2007, Elashi and six fellow HLF leaders were charged with twelve counts of providing "material support and resources" to a foreign terrorist organization, Hamas. Additionally, they faced thirteen counts of money laundering and thirteen counts of breaching the International Emergency Economic Powers Act, which prohibits transactions that threaten American national security. Along with the seven named defendants, the government released a list of approximately 300 "unindicted co-conspirators" and "joint venturers."[138]

On November 24, 2008, a jury convicted Elashi and four other former HLF officials of conspiring to provide

---

[138] "Ghassan Elashi." Discover the Networks."
http://www.discoverthenetworks.org/individualProfile.asp?indid=729

material support to terrorists. Elashi was sentenced to 65 years in prison.

CAIR denies any responsibility, because "the fact that Elashi was once briefly associated with one of our more than 30 regional chapters has no legal significance to our corporation." Briefly associated with a chapter? He *founded* a chapter.[139]

Rabih Haddad - Haddad served as a fundraiser for a CAIR chapter in Ann Arbor, Michigan.

In the 1990s he had worked with Makhtab al-Khidamat, a group founded by Abdullah Azzam (a founding member of al-Qaeda), Osama Bin Laden and current al-Qaeda leader Ayman al-Zawahiri to raise money to fight the Soviet Union in Afghanistan.

In December 2002, Elashi was charged with "selling computers and computer parts to Libya and Syria, both designated state sponsors of terrorism."

Before he was charged and jailed, the Revolutionary Communist Party (there's a 100% chance you've seen a protester holding a sign with their RevCom website advertised on it before) published an article in March of 2002 documenting Haddad's "nightmare in post-9/11 America." They noted that 5,000 people have signed a petition demanding his release. Yes - he's the victim here to them.[140]

---

[139] "Top Internet Misinformation and Conspiracy Theories About CAIR." CAIR, March 11, 2015. https://www.cair.com/about-us/dispelling-rumors-about-cair.html

[140] "Rabih Haddad's Nightmare in Post 9/11 America." Revolutionary Worker #1144, March 24, 2002. http://revcom.us/a/v23/1140-1147/1144/rabih%20haddad.htm

He was deported to Lebanon with his family in July 2003.

Muthanna Al-Hanooti - Al-Hanooti first worked for CAIR National in Washington, then headed their Michigan office. He's related to Sheik Mohammed al-Hanooti, one of the many unindicted conspirators in the 1993 WTC bombing.

The FBI alleges Mohammed al-Hanooti, an ethnic-Palestinian who also emigrated from Iraq, raised money for Hamas. In fact, "al-Hanooti collected over $6 million for support of Hamas," according to a 2001 FBI report, and was present with CAIR and Holy Land Foundation officials at a secret Hamas fundraising summit held last decade at a Philadelphia hotel.[141]

His trial and charges were actually unrelated from his alleged Hamas financing however. He was sentenced to a year in prison for illegally attempting to purchase oil from the Iraqi government despite sanctions.[142]

Nabil Sadoun - Sadoun was a member of CAIR's national board of directors, serving as their vice chairman before being deported in 2010. He began working at CAIR in 1996.

Three years before joining CAIR, in a 1993 interview he was asked a question concerning the Palestinian-Israeli conflict. Jews, he said, "are the first priority for Muslim[s] until the Holy Land is liberated and the backbone of the Jews is broken." He then cited Qur'an 5:82, which he said was "God Almighty's most accurate description of Jews." The

---

[141] "Ex-CAIR Official Sentenced To Prison." World Net Daily, March 19, 2011. http://www.wnd.com/2011/03/277349/

[142] Hawkins, Derek. "Ex-Charity Official Gets 1 Year For Iraq Oil Deal." Law 260, March 18, 2011.
https://www.law360.com/articles/233131/ex-charity-official-gets-1-year-for-iraq-oil-deal

verse states that "**You will surely find the most intense of the people in animosity toward the believers [to be] the Jews and those who associate others with Allah.**" (A translation that's in more modern english reads "**Certainly you will find the most violent of people in enmity for those who believe (to be) the Jews and those who are polytheists**"

He also was in frequent contact with Khalid Mishal (a Hamas member who became their chairman in 1996), with phone records obtained through a FOIA request after his deportation documenting a dozen calls between the two from 1993-94.[143]

That didn't prevent him from employment at CAIR (and honestly, it probably helped).

He was deported for failing to attend an immigrant hearing in Dallas. Files in his deportation case state that he was a member of American Hamas support efforts. He ran an organization called MAYA, with the FBI stating that it "served as a conduit for money to Hamas... and served as a forum where Hamas could promote its ideology and recruit new members."[144]

Prior to his (forced) departure from CAIR, his bio on their website informed us that "Dr. Sadoun's interests also include educating Americans about the true teachings and image of Islam, combating extremism and stereotypes, and

---

[143] "FOIA Exposes Deported CAIR Official's Support for Jihad." IPT News, December 14, 2015.
https://www.investigativeproject.org/5089/foia-exposes-deported-cair-official-support-for
[144] Ibid.

promoting an environment of mutual understanding among Muslims and other nations."

Believe it or not, the FBI once had a close relationship with CAIR, but later cut those ties in 2008 due to the 2007 Holy Land Foundation trial, in which evidence was provided linking CAIR leaders to Hamas. CAIR was named as an unindicted conspirator in the case.[145] As part of those ties being cut, when the FBI sponsors community outreach programs with the Muslim community, they will not attend personally if even a single CAIR-affiliated individual is present.

Keith Ellison

CAIR's de-facto representative in Congress is Keith Ellison, the first Muslim to be elected to Congress (and only one of two in Congress, Andrew Carson being the other).

The man clearly has a little bit of Farrakhan in him, given his black nationalist past. When he was elected to Congress in 2006 he had to try to explain away his Nation of Islam ties - presumably for publicity purposes. "I have long since distanced myself from and rejected the Nation of Islam due to its propagation of bigoted and anti-Semitic statements and actions of the Nation of Islam, Louis Farrakhan, and [Farrakhan's late assistant] Khalid Muhammed" he wrote in a letter to a local chapter of the Jewish Community Relations Council, who understandably expressed concern over his views.

---

[145] "Executive Summary: Review of FBI Interactions with the Council on American-Islamic Relations." U.S. Department of Justice, September 2013. https://oig.justice.gov/reports/2013/e0707r-summary.pdf

So what were some of these past views of his that he had to distance himself from? A number of questionable statements he made in the Minnesota Daily when he was a law student at the University of Minnesota in the 80s.

Ellison's official defense is that his involvement with the Nation of Islam was confined to an 18-month period around the time of the Million Man March in 1995 (a gathering of African-Americans at the National Mall organized by Farrakhan), but his columns clearly show that he was at least sympathetic to the group long before then. As The Weekly Standard's Scott Johnson discovered following Ellison's electoral victory:

As a third-year student at the University of Minnesota Law School in 1989-90, he wrote two columns for the *Minnesota Daily* under the name "Keith Hakim." In the first, Ellison refers to "Minister Louis Farrakhan," defends Nation of Islam spokesman Khalid Abdul Muhammad, and speaks in the voice of a Nation of Islam advocate. In the second, "Hakim" demands reparations for slavery and throws in a demand for an optional separate homeland for American blacks.[146]

The columns also advocate for cash reparations to be paid from whites to blacks, and describes the U.S. Constitution as the "best evidence of a white racist conspiracy to subjugate other peoples." The Nation of Islam is also praised for their "most notable results" in fighting the problem of drug use.

---

[146] Johnson, Scott W. "Louis Farrakhan's First Congressman." The Weekly Standard, October 9, 2006.
http://www.weeklystandard.com/louis-farrakhans-brfirst-congressman/article/13892

The motivation for his defense of the Nation came after the school's Africana Student Cultural Center began sponsoring speeches by Farrakhan, sparking tension between Muslims and Jews on campus.

Among the Center's most controversial speakers they invited to campus was Kwame Ture, a Black Panther who gave a speech in which he attacked Zionism as a form of white supremacy. I'm sure actual Nazis would be thrilled to have Zionism lumped in with their beliefs.

Introducing Ture was none other than Keith Ellison. Unfortunately the only video recording of the event cuts off just a few sentences in his introduction (after referring to the "honorable Louis Farrakhan).[147]

But back to the student paper. Michael Olenick, a Jewish student, served as the Minnesota Daily's opinion editor from 1989-1990. When interviewed by Mother Jones, he recalled his opposition to publishing Ellison's columns under his pseudonym Keith Hakim. Ellison claimed to have been in the process of legally changing his name to Hakim (and clearly hasn't made much progress).

But that wasn't all.

Olenick recalled Ellison maintaining that an oppressed group could not be racist toward Jews because Jews were themselves oppressors. "European white Jews are trying to oppress minorities all over the world," Olenick remembers Ellison arguing. "Keith would go on all the time about 'Jewish slave traders.'" Another Jewish student active in progressive politics recalled Ellison's incredulous

---

[147] You can find the lecture on YouTube:
https://www.youtube.com/watch?v=yQrDBZfDjZA

response to the controversy over Zionism. "What are you afraid of?" Ellison asked. "Do you think black nationalists are gonna get power and hurt Jews?"[148]

If Ellison can be credited for anything, it's for being ahead of the social justice curve on the "power plus prejudice" cliché.

By February of 1997 (within his 18-month timeframe), Ellison was a local spokesman for the Nation of Islam, and his connection to the group continued after he claimed to have made a clean break.

In 1998, when Ellison (then going by Keith-Muhammad) first was a political candidate, Insight News reported that "Anticipating possible criticism for his NOI affiliation, Ellison-Muhammad says he is aware that not everyone appreciates what the Nation does and feels there is a propaganda war being launched against its leader, Minister Louis Farrakhan."[149]

All this information was brought to light when Ellison initially ran for Congress, then again when he was in the running to head the DNC after Debbie Wasserman Schultz. Liberals were more than happy to present the story as if Ellison was being "smeared." And of course, those merely reporting the facts were "Islamophobes" for doing so.

Since when is something a "smear" when it's true?

---

[148] Murphy, Tim. "Keith Ellison is Everything Republicans Thought Obama Was. Maybe He's Just What Democrats Need." Mother Jones, March/April 2017 Issue.
http://www.motherjones.com/politics/2017/02/keith-ellison-democratic-national-committee-chair
[149] Johnson, Weekly Standard.

The Spectre of Non-Existent Christian (or Right-Wing) Terrorism

Is there a single person who has pointed out the problem of Islamic terrorism only to be told about "Christian terrorism"? Just remember the crusades, they'll tell you.

When the only argument they can conjure up involves blurring history 700+ years ago with the present, it should be a hint that they don't really have an argument. Most days, we don't have to look back more than a week in history to cite an example of Islamic terror. It also neglects the entire fact that the crusades were in response to Islamic imperialism, but that's a subject that could fill up an entire other book.

OK - but what about something like abortion clinic bombings? In the entire history of legal abortion in America there have been 11 people murdered in anti-abortion related violence, the majority (seven) occurring in the 1990s.[150] Eleven deaths are what a jihadist calls "a bad day."

Anyone who considers abortion to be murder can glean from this that abortion doctors have the highest kill-death ratio of all time.

Another favorite talking point is to point to other forms of terrorism, presumably to make the case that any ideology has its crazies. The libertarian Cato Institute (who really ought to know better), for instance, quotes a Government Accountability Report that states "of the 85 violent extremist incidents that resulted in death since

---

[150] "Violence Statistics & History." National Abortion Federation. https://prochoice.org/education-and-advocacy/violence/violence-statistics-and-history

September 12, 2001, far right wing violent extremist groups were responsible for 62 (73 percent) while radical Islamist violent extremists were responsible for 23 (27 percent)."[151]

So right off the bat we're told that in absence of the worst terror attack on American soil, right wing extremists have committed more attacks. Of course, had 9/11 been counted, it wouldn't have changed the results, because it would've only counted as one incident.

So let's look at the numbers. The GAO report cites 225 deaths from Islamist and far-right ideologies over their time frame. The Pulse nightclub shooting killed 49, the San Bernardino shootings killed 14, the Fort Hood shooting killed 14 - so we're a mere three Islamic attacks in and those alone are responsible for a third of all terrorist fatalities. The split, according to the study, is 106 deaths attributable to far-right extremists in 62 different incidents, and 119 victims of Islamic terrorism in 23 incidents. Far-right extremists don't even average two kills per terror attack, while Islamic extremists average nearly five.

Frequency of attacks is meaningless when the perpetrators are about as effective as a North Korean missile. Regardless, most of those in the "right-wing terror" category are crimes that really ought to be classified as hate crimes, as nearly every single attack documented involves a Neo-Nazi or white supremacist attacking usually a single person.[152] For example, one of these "right wing terror attacks" documented by the GAO literally reads "White

---

[151] "GAO Weighs In On "Countering Violent Extremism." Cato Institute, April 13, 2017.
https://www.cato.org/blog/gao-weighs-countering-violent-extremism
[152] "Countering Violent Extremism." Government Accountability Office, April 2017. http://www.gao.gov/assets/690/683984.pdf. See pages 29-32 for the list of "right wing" attacks.

supremacist murdered his stepfather to gain street cred." Horrible, yes, but right wing terrorism? Hardly.

One of the most deadly "right-wing" attacks (nine dead) included on the GAO's list was a mass public shooting at Umpqua Community College in which the shooter targeted Christians. The GAO report describes the shooter as a "white supremacist," but there's no evidence whatsoever that his crime was motivated by those beliefs. The shooter's Facebook page at the time of the shooting described himself as "mixed-race."

Even though nearly every single "right-wing terror attack" documented by the GAO is a hate crime, not a terror attack, above all, you'd think those employed at Cato, in relaying the information, would recognize that there are one-hell of a lot more people in America with right-wing, or even views that could be classified as "far-right/extremist right," than there are Muslims in America, who make up about a percent of the population.

Regardless, let's not forget that terrorism is a global problem. There were 29,376 terror deaths in 2015. We could get a much larger number if we applied Government Accountability Office logic and classified honor killings as acts of Islamic terror. Anyway, of those nearly-30,000 deaths, seventy-two percent of them were in just five countries: Iraq, Afghanistan, Pakistan, India, and Nigeria, with four Islamist groups responsible for 74 percent of the attacks: ISIS, Boko Haram (ISIS-affiliated), the Taliban, and al-Qaeda.[153] Nearly a third of terror deaths (11,900) are concentrated in both Iraq and Nigeria, where ISIS and ISIS-

[153] "Global Terrorism Index: 2016." Institute for Economics and Peace, November 2016. http://economicsandpeace.org/wp-content/uploads/2016/11/Global-Terrorism-Index-2016.2.pdf

affiliate Boko Haram are responsible for nearly all terror deaths.

Of the twenty most dangerous attacks in 2015, with death tolls ranging from 80 per attack to 300 per attack, all but two were carried out by Islamist militants.[154]

Liberal Explanations for Islamic Terrorism

A satirical video from The Onion comes to mind whenever I see liberals making excuse for Islamic terrorism: "'9/11 Conspiracy Theories Ridiculous' - Al Qaeda." In it, a man playing an al-Qaeda member debates a man playing a 9/11 truther, expressing frustration that the terror group isn't getting the credit they rightfully deserve.

And it didn't take long for The Onion to become reality on that issue, but thanks to the many excuses liberals make for them, not conspiracy theorists.

Following the Pulse Nightclub shooting in Orlando, in which the worst mass public shooting in American history was carried out at the gay nightclub on their Latino night by ISIS inspired Omar Mateen, everything except Islam was blamed.

The most logical explanation for liberals? That the shooter Omar Mateen was inspired by homophobia - which is probably true, it's just that liberals are unable to identify the source of that homophobia. Or perhaps it was an anti-Latino

---

[154] The two non-Islamic attacks weren't carried out by right-wing extremists either, they were carried out by Fulani militants (who, while they aren't explicitly an Islamist organization, have been documented killing Christians in attempts to Islamize the regions they control), and the other was an attack assisted by the communist Donetsk People's Republic.

hate crime! The fact that Mateen pledged allegiance to ISIS and a handful of other terror groups in a 9/11 call during the attack, and that he was twice investigated by the FBI in the past for potential terror ties were irrelevant to the media narrative.

Conservatives weren't the only ones pointing out the ridiculousness of the situation. Al-Qaeda responded to the confusion by encouraging their lone wolf attackers to start targeting whites to avoid the "hate crime" label. Their "Inspire Magazine" ran a special Orlando edition in which they praised the attacks.

It also included the following "advice":

> The executer specifically chose a homosexual nightclub, and even though the killing of such people is the most binding duty and closer to human nature, but better than this is to avoid targeting areas where minorities are found. This is in order not to deviate the essence of the operation and letting it be termed as a small issue as the American media is trying to portray in the case of Mateen. The Western media focused on the testimony by Mateen's father who said that his son hates homosexuals and that terrorist ideas had no place in his motives. The media reiterated this, saying that Umar saw some homosexuals kissing each other and that such a scene offended him. **The media tried to portray the operation motives to be against a particular group of people in order to turn the American public away from the real motives of the operation.**[155]

---

[155] "Inspire Guide: Orlando Operation." Inspire Magazine. https://azelin.files.wordpress.com/2016/06/al-qacc84_idah-in-the-arabian-peninsula-22inspire-guide-orlando-operation22.pdf

If Al-Qaeda isn't buying your excuses for terrorism, perhaps it's time to revise them.

But that all being said, let's look at all the other explanations for extremism.

Poverty, Deprivation, Desperation

Could it be poverty and desperation driving people to extremism? We'll ignore that it hasn't in any other religions, and look right at the data.

The question to answer is simply "Who are the world's terrorists, and where do they come from?" Among those we have data on, it ain't from the world's slums. Here's a look at the facts:

-        A study of 331 ISIS recruits from the World Bank found that 69% had at least a   high school education, while at least a quarter were college educated. Less than 2% of terrorists are illiterate.[156]

-        A 2007 Oxford study of 326 terrorists in the Middle East and North Africa found that nearly half were college education, and 44% of the college educated had engineering degrees. Fifty-two of the 81 top leaders in Hamas were college educated at the time of the study. The more educated a terrorist is, the more likely they are to be a suicide bomber.[157]

---

[156] Meotti, Giulio. "Islamic Terrorists not Poor and Illiterate, but Rich and Educated." The Gatestone Institute, November 19, 2016.
https://www.gatestoneinstitute.org/9343/terrorism-poverty-despair
[157] MacDonald, Elizabeth. "Study Shows Technical College Degrees Make Ideal Terrorists. Fox News, December 9, 2015.
http://www.foxbusiness.com/features/2015/12/09/study-shows-technical-college-degrees-make-ideal-terrorists.html

-       The richer the country is, the more likely they are to provide foreign recruits to ISIS.

-       A study of 160 families whose children left France to wage Jihad in Syria by the Center for Prevention, Deradicalization and Individual Monitoring found that two thirds were members of the middle class.

-       According to Britain's M15 (intelligence agency), two thirds of British terror suspects fit a middle-class profile.[158]

-       According to a survey of British Muslims, less than 3 percent were sympathetic with terrorism, however, those most likely to be sympathetic were born in the UK, under the age of 20, and full time students. Another demographic prone to support terrorism were those from high-income homes (over $123,000 a year). "We were surprised that [the] inequality paradigm seems not to be supported," the lead researcher behind the study told Al-Jazeera.[159]

---

[158] Taher, Abul. "The middle-class terrorists: more than 60pc of suspects are well educated and from comfortable backgrounds, says secret M15 file." The Daily Mail, October 15, 2011.
http://www.dailymail.co.uk/news/article-2049646/The-middle-class-terrorists-More-60pc-suspects-educated-comfortable-backgrounds-says-secret-M15-file.html
[159] "Younger, Educated and Affluent – The UK's Terror Sympathizers." The Investigative Project on Terrorism, March 20, 2014.
https://www.investigativeproject.org/4322/younger-educated-and-affluent-the-uk-terror

It's no wonder that current Al-Qaeda leader Ayman al-Zawahiri (who himself has a degree in Medicine) boasted "the Islamist movement had found its greatest recruiting success in the university's two most élite faculties—the medical and engineering schools."[160]

Meanwhile, even those with political power pretend the opposite to be the case. John Kerry referred to "poverty and deprivation" as the "root cause of terrorism."

Then again, remember that he's the man who couldn't even defeat George W. Bush.

Speaking of Bush, two-thirds of the 25 terrorists involved in the planning and hijacking on 9/11 had attended University.[161]

Result of American foreign policy (blowback, occupation, and other excuses)

Completely ignoring that Islamic terrorism (or at least Islamic violence) is as old as Islam itself, it's a common talking point among liberals (and even many non-interventionists on the Right) that we in America are responsible for terrorism. Why? "Blowback" as the Ron Pauls of the world call it.

There's no war without casualties, so according to the blowback theory, we end up creating more terrorists than we can kill. Suppose we kill a terrorist - but during the attack a handful of innocent civilians are killed. The family of those

---

[160] "Study Shows Technical College Degrees Make Ideal Terrorists. Fox News.
[161] Bergen, Peter and Swati Pandey. "The Madrassa Myth." The New York Times, June 14, 2005.
http://www.nytimes.com/2005/06/14/opinion/the-madrassa-myth.html

civilians we kill are going to be radicalized against the West, wanting revenge.[162]

For as much as the Left is against victim blaming, they seem happy to blame the victim so long as it's the West. Noam Chomsky, who is widely regarded an intellectual for reasons not yet discovered, blames 9/11 (and subsequent attacks) on American occupation of foreign lands, stating "They [the Jihadists] have more attacks against us and the American interests per month than occurred in all the years before 9/11. But we're there, occupying their land. And if we think that we can do that and not have retaliation, we're kidding ourselves."[163]

"Terrorism in Paris: Blowback for Yet Another Unnecessary War" read one headline on the libertarian Cato Institute, in which the author tried to blame the Paris Bataclan Nightclub massacre on France beginning to bomb ISIS fourteen months prior.[164]

So what's the logic here? We let terrorists continue to commit genocide because they won't like us when we kill them? "What causes terrorism is our resistance to it" appears to be the argument here.

The late Christopher Hitchens mocked this kind of logic perfectly in a debate with George Galloway, (and I'm

---

[162] Indeed, there was so much "blowback" against America from our occupation of Iraq that the overwhelming majority of Iraqi civilians killed were killed by sectarian (Sunni vs. Shia) violence.

[163] "Noam Chomsky: 'Ron Paul Was Right About 9/11 Motive.'" September 13, 2011. http://readersupportednews.org/opinion2/291-144/7390-noam-chomsky-qron-paul-was-right-about-911-motiveq

[164] Bandow, Doug. "Terrorism in Paris: Blowback for Yet Another Unnecessary War." The Cato Institute, November 23, 2015. https://www.cato.org/blog/terrorism-paris-blowback-yet-another-unnecessary-war

paraphrasing) that we'd have to believe these sociopaths who have no trouble stoning women to death for being raped, beheading nonbelievers, and carrying out acts of terror, wouldn't be this way if only America wasn't so mean to them.

Does that make sense to you? It shouldn't. The logic of blowback makes sense on the surface, and could certainly explain why someone would want to cause harm to America, but the overwhelming majority of terror attacks kill other Muslims. Why do that if they're angry at America for our foreign policy?

Can anyone imagine what chain of events would have to take place for the blowback hypothesis to be true?

Imagine, a Pakistani man's family was just accidentally killed as collateral damage in a drone strike. The probability that his next thought is "I'm going to shoot Malala for wanting to get an education" is about zero.

Ironically, Malala herself has made the argument that the more you criticize Islam, the more you're likely to create terrorists, which I believe roughly translates to "don't criticize Muslims or they will kill you."

But enough mockery, onto the evidence.

A study published in the International Journal of Conflict Management that examined the effects of drone strikes in Pakistan found, quite unsurprisingly, that killing terrorists by incinerating them from the skies tends to both reduce the supply of terrorists - and not contribute to a net increase in new terrorists through "blowback."

To quote from the abstract:

Focusing on remotely piloted aerial vehicle (RPV) strikes in Pakistan over 2008 to 2013, the analysis yields important new insights. The principal **finding suggests that RPVs reduce overall terrorism, while, without negating the negative spillover effects of RPVs use**, there is no evidence of a positive feedback from civilian casualties to terrorism.[165]

And that's hardly the only study reaching that conclusion. A study from a researcher at the RAND corporation and the University of Minnesota examined the impact of U.S drone strikes in Pakistan from 2007-2011, concluding that "drone strikes are associated with decreases in the incidence and lethality of terrorist attacks," and that, "the results do lend some credence to the argument that drone strikes, while unpopular, have bolstered counter-terrorism efforts in Pakistan."[166]

Obviously these benefits need to be weighed against the costs of civilian casualties, but drone strikes do cause fewer civilian casualties per enemy combatant killed than boots on the ground.

Of course, this doesn't mean there aren't cases in which good intentions can go awry.

---

[165] Ummad Mazhar, (2016) "Do remotely piloted aerial vehicles make terrorism more costly for terrorists?: Empirical evidence from Pakistan", International Journal of Conflict Management, Vol. 27 Issue: 4, pp.470-486, doi: 10.1108/IJCMA-06-2015-0035

[166] Johnston, Patrick B. and Anoop K. Sarhabi. "The Impact of U.S. Drone Strikes On Terrorism In Pakistan." International Studies Quarterly. http://patrickjohnston.info/materials/drones.pdf

Seung-Whan Cho's paper "Does U.S. Military Intervention Reduce or Increase Terrorism?" at the University of Illinois at Chicago used a cross-national, time-series analysis of 166 countries during the period from 1970 to 2005 and found that the overall effect of U.S. military intervention on terrorism is detrimental, fueling more terrorist incidents if not more terrorist casualties.

However, and this is a big however, he also found that "Terrorist pursuit interventions successfully deter terrorism, but other intervention missions, such as those that neutralize domestic disputes, facilitate regime change, and offer humanitarian aid, backfire. These findings indicate that the U.S. should be more cautious of the use of the military since it inflames terrorism except for those instances in which combating terrorism is set as a central goal."[167]

Thus, while broader military interventions may result in more terrorism, while killing terrorists on net creates fewer terrorists, not more. As it turns out, one minus one equals zero after all.

"Every Religion Has Its Crazies"

We've all heard the deflection strategy following an act of Islamic terror. Christianity has been just as bad in the past we'll be reminded, after all, "just look at the Crusades!"

Memo to those making this argument: when you have to blend the present with historical events a millennium ago, it may be time to revise your argument.

---

[167] Choi, Seung-Whan, Does U.S. Military Intervention Reduce or Increase Terrorism? (2011). APSA 2011 Annual Meeting Paper. Available at SSRN: https://ssrn.com/abstract=1900375

Anyway, let's ignore the fact that yes, we can find an example of an extremist or two in nearly every religion, and instead look at the overall numbers. Is Islam overrepresented when it comes to motivation to cause terror? You bet.

Earlier I discussed terror attacks in America and globally, noting that even if we use a timeframe favorable to liberals (post-9/11, that is), the statistics still don't say what they want them too. And looking at the numbers again, I'll also be looking at the overall death toll, not the frequency of attacks deemed terror. To better understand why, look at U.S. terror attacks from 1980-2005 and you'll find that only 6% of terror attacks were carried out by Muslims (the largest being Latino groups at 42%, and extreme left wing groups with 24%) - but that mere 6% killed more than the other 94% combined.[168]

Not a single other death could be attributed to another religiously-motivated terrorist organization, though there were deaths that could be classified as religiously motivated. Among them are the 1994 murder of abortion doctor Dr. John Britton, the 1996 Centennial Olympic Park bombing, and 1998 murder of abortion doctor Barnett Slepian), but that's only three deaths.

To paraphrase Sam Harris, if a religion has good fundamentals - it's fundamentalists will be good people, and as Sam Harris puts it, the problem with fundamentalist Islam is the fundamentals of Islam.

---

[168] "Terrorism 2002-2005." Department of Justice/FBI.
https://www.fbi.gov/stats-services/publications/terrorism-2002-2005#terror_05sum While the title of the page is about attacks "2002-2005" a longer timeline of statistics is available near the bottom of hte page.

ISIS: Why We Hate You

So why do the terrorists hate us? Apparently nobody ever thought to ask a terrorist that question.

Just like Al-Qaeda does, ISIS has a media arm that releases a magazine, called "Dabiq," named after a Syrian city where they believe they'll bring on the apocalypse. The 15th issue of the magazine ran an article titled "Why We Hate You & Why We Fight You."[169]

Are they mad about our foreign policy? Of course they are - because it thwarts their goals, but their goals of conquest would remain in place regardless of what America does.

The article begins by mocking the response from our media and politicians to the aforementioned Pulse Nightclub shooting. "Shortly following the blessed attack on a sodomite" the article begins, "American politicians were quick to jump in the spotlight and denounce the shooting, declaring it a hate crime, an act of terrorism, and an act of senseless violence."

"A hate crime?" ISIS asked, "Yes. Muslims undoubtedly hate liberalist sodomites, as does anyone else with any shred of their fitrah (inborn human nature) still intact."

So ridiculous was the excuse making, ISIS wrote that "One would think that the average Westerner, by now, would have abandoned the tired claim that the actions of the

---

[169] Dabiq, Issue 15: Break the Cross.https://azelin.files.wordpress.com/2016/07/the-islamic-state-e2809cdacc84biq-magazine-1522.pdf

mujahidin - who have repeatedly stated their goals, intentions, and motivations - don't make sense."

No kidding.

They then lay out six bullet points explaining why they hate us, and accurately predict that despite laying out their motives in plain English, Western politicians will lie about them.

Here they are, condensed:

1. We hate you, first and foremost, because you are disbelievers; you reject the oneness of Allah – whether you realize it or not – by making partners for Him in worship, you blaspheme against Him, claiming that He has a son, you fabricate lies against His prophets and messengers, and you indulge in all manner of devilish practices.

And the key passage under that bullet point:

...**even if you were to stop fighting us, your best-case scenario in a state of war would be that we would suspend our attacks against you – if we deemed it necessary – in order to focus on the closer and more immediate threats, before eventually resuming our campaigns against you.** Apart from the option of a temporary truce, this is the only likely scenario that would bring you fleeting respite from our attacks. So in the end, you cannot bring an indefinite halt to our war against you. At most, you could only delay it temporarily

2. We hate you because your secular, liberal societies permit the very things that Allah has prohibited while

banning many of the things He has permitted, a matter that doesn't concern you because you separate between religion and state, thereby granting supreme authority to your whims and desires via the legislators you vote into power. In doing so, you desire to rob Allah of His right to be obeyed and you wish to usurp that right for yourselves. "Legislation is not but for Allah" (Yusuf 40). **Your secular liberalism has led you to tolerate and even support "gay rights," to allow alcohol, drugs, fornication, gambling, and usury to become widespread**, and to encourage the people to mock those who denounce these filthy sins and vices.

That section of the article is accompanied with a photo of a child holding a sign that reads "My 2 Moms Are Married!"

The rest of their explanations are much of the same, complaining that they don't like that we thwart their sociopathic goals.

3. In the case of the atheist fringe, we hate you and wage war against you because you disbelieve in the existence of your Lord and Creator.
4. We hate you for your crimes against Islam and wage war against you to punish you for your transgressions against our religion.
5. We hate you for your crimes against the Muslims; your drones and fighter jets bomb, kill, and maim our people around the world, and your puppets in the usurped lands of the Muslims oppress, torture, and wage war against anyone who calls to the truth.
6. We hate you for invading our lands and fight you to repel you and drive you out. As long as there is an inch of territory left for us to reclaim, jihad will continue to be a personal obligation on every single Muslim.

While their last few reasons do appear to lend some credibility to the liberal narrative, ISIS is quick to clarify **"that although some might argue that your foreign policies are the extent of what drives our hatred, this particular reason for hating you is secondary**, hence the reason we addressed it at the end of the above list. **The fact is, even if you were to stop bombing us, imprisoning us, torturing us, vilifying us, and usurping our lands, we would continue to hate you because our primary reason for hating you will not cease to exist until you embrace Islam.** Even if you were to pay jizyah and live under the authority of Islam in humiliation, we would continue to hate you. No doubt, we would stop fighting you then as we would stop fighting any disbelievers who enter into a covenant with us, **but we would not stop hating you."**

Well, that settles that.

Islamophobia Insanity

In 2010, a national debate erupted after what was dubbed the "Ground Zero Mosque" was proposed. Officially called the Cordoba House, then Park 51, the proposed structure would've replaced an existing building damaged in the 9/11 attacks. Among the features of the building, which was presented by proponents as a "community center" would've included an Islamic prayer space of between 1000-2000 square fett (out of a total 8,000 sq. ft. in the entire building) hence the "ground zero mosque" nickname.

As you'd imagine, most people opposed the mosque (most polls showed between 60-70% opposition), and of course, the majority must've been "Islamophobic," rather than just feeling a little dismayed over the location of the proposed mosque.

TIME Magazine ran a cover bearing the question "Is America Islamophobic?" in August 2010, reflecting the latest bigotry buzzword the Left had to hurl at their enemies. But are they right? A quick look at the data yields the answer; not really.

Below is tabled the frequency of anti-Jewish and anti-Muslim hate crimes in America each year. Jews and Muslims both compose a similar percentage of the American population, hence why I'm comparing those two religious groups and not including the statistics for anti-Catholic or anti-Protestant crimes.[170]

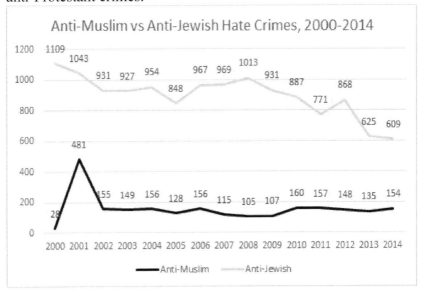

Next, let's look at anti-Jewish and anti-Muslim hate crimes as a percentage of all religiously motivated hate crimes.

[170] "Comparison of FBI Hate Crime Statistics, 2000-2014." Anti-Defamation League.
https://www.adl.org/sites/default/files/documents/assets/pdf/combating-hate/FBI-Hate-Crime-Statistics-Comparison-2000-2014DK-2.pdf

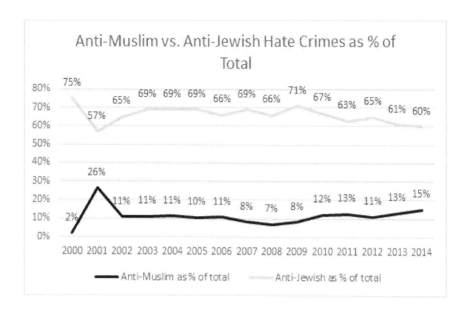

Anti-Muslim vs. Anti-Jewish Hate Crimes as % of Total

Granted, one could (rightly) argue that Muslims are still hate crime victims far out of proportion to their share of the national population (3.3 million in 2016, or about 1% of the total US pop), but the average of 155 hate crimes a year (less if you exclude 2001 as an outlier year) amounts to a rate of 4.7 per 100,000 Muslims.

One is too many, but that's hardly epidemic proportions, and it sure as hell doesn't reflect the claims out of grievance mongers like Linda Sarsour who claim that Muslims are being killed in the streets in America.[171]

Those portraying what they deem "Islamophobic" (anything critical of Islam) as a form of racism need to be reminded that not only is Islam not a race, but that anti-Islam sentiments are not driven by perceptions that Muslims are arab. Anti-Islam beliefs are by and large driven by their

---

[171] The Rachel Maddow Show, February 18, 2015.

obvious conflict with Western values (which are discussed in greater length in Chapter Nine).

A study published in Political Psychology in March 2017 had a clever way of analyzing this. The researchers conducted two experiments in which they aimed to measure a participant's likelihood to help a Muslim and non-Muslim in an action that was either neutral or possibly conflicting with Western values.

And the results? When the cause the Muslim needed a helping hand with was neutral (such as needing help making copies of something, or needing help researching how to visit a relative abroad), there was no bias in treatment between the Muslim and the non-Muslim.[172]

However, when the causes conflicted with Western values (such as protesting against a headscarf ban, or were for an anti-gay cause), people were more reluctant to help the Muslim person promoting those causes.

In conclusion, the study found significant evidence against the hypothesis that there's general anti-Muslim prejudice.

Now, to briefly address the claim that Islamophobia is somehow driving people to terrorism, that's dispelled by the fact that nearly all terrorists originate from the Muslim world.

---

[172] Van der Noll, Vassilis Saroglou, David Latour, and Nathalie Dolezal. "Western Anti-Muslim Prejudice: Value Conflict or Discrimination of Persons Too?" Political Psychology, 2017. http://onlinelibrary.wiley.com/doi/10.1111/pops.12416/full

CHAPTER EIGHT
Islam on Campus: BDS B.S.

One of the most popular anti-Israel movements on college campuses is the BDS - Boycott, Divest, and Sanction - movement. Who are they? In their words, the BDS "movement works to end international support for Israel's oppression of Palestinians and pressure Israel to comply with international law." They're also strongly against "Israeli apartheid."

Of course, some translation is in order. The BDS movement works to pressure, threaten, and protest any business that would dare operate in Israel (even if they employ mostly Palestinians), and hold Israel to a standard that no other country is held to.

I bring up this parody of a civil rights movement only because it highlights the far-left's willingness to betray liberal principles in defense of whatever bizarre cause they're championing.

Take the BDS movement's economic boycotts as an example. The Israeli company SodaStream faced enormous international pressure thanks to BDS to withdraw their presence from the "occupied West Bank." The historical fact that Israel began occupying the West Bank after being attacked by Jordan in 1967 was irrelevant - as is the fact Israel did try to give the West Bank back to the Palestinians in 2000 and 2008.... which they rejected. For Israel's sake, thank God they did, as we know what happens when Israel does give land back (such as the Gaza Strip). They're given a huge "thank you" in the form of a hail of rocket fire from Hamas.

The company's CEO Daniel Birnbaum said that they left the West Bank because of a consolidation plan they already had in place - but in absence of BDS they would've stayed for another year or two. In the end, 500 Palestinians ended up losing their jobs. Take that Israel!

There are plenty of individual examples that could be cited, but the larger point is that Palestine's economy is largely dependent on Israel's. You cannot hurt Israel without causing damage to the Palestinian people. Heck, even working conditions for the 120,000 Palestinians working in Israeli companies are more favorable than Palestinians working in Palestinian companies. And things would be even better - if it wasn't for the patriarchal culture in Palestine.

Palestine Media Watch captured an exchange I was shocked to see aired on Palestinian television, in which the guest admitted as much.

Attorney Khaled Al-Doukhi: Israeli labor law is a very good law regarding workers' rights, for both men and women. Israeli law does not differentiate between a worker who has entered Israel illegally or legally... Unfortunately, even though it is very good, in practice, the law has become very bad for female Palestinian workers. For instance, the Palestinian female workers in the agricultural sector enjoy many rights, like any Israeli worker in the agricultural sector: The salary is higher than the minimum wage, 14 vacation days a year in the first four years, 2,000 shekels convalescence pay [yearly] in the first year and 2,200 shekels in the second and third year for every worker in Israel, payment for holidays, whether Islamic or Jewish. It is a matter of choice."

TV host: "But in practice, do they enjoy these rights provided by law?"

Attorney Khaled Al-Doukhi of Worker's Hotline: "In reality, Palestinian workers – and especially the female Palestinian workers – do not receive these things. Why? You said: "The Palestinian middleman deducts from her [salary]." No, he does not deduct, he shares her salary. In practice, he takes 50 percent, 60 percent, and even 70 percent of her salary. If her daily salary is 180 shekels, in the end she receives 60 shekels. The middleman steals two thirds of her salary. Excuse the word ["steals"], but that is the exact word."[173]

No outrage from BDS over that one yet.

The kooks in BDS are the kind of people who see that the United Nations passed five times more human rights violations against Israel in 2016 than they did to Syria, Russia, Iran, North Korea, and the rest of the world combined and think to themselves that Israel sure must be really sinister. Israel - not Saudi Arabia, Iran, Afghanistan, Pakistan, Sudan, or Somalia was the only country in the world that was named a violator of women's rights.[174] You'd think something like confiscating only women's salaries for working in Israel would conjure up with a violation too.

Is there truly any doubt that Israel is at least the freest place in the Middle East? For anyone reading this who is a woman, gay, secular, transgender, or non-Muslim, can you name what country other than Israel in the Middle-East that

---

[173] Arutz Sheva Staff. "Why do Palestinians Prefer to Work for Israeli Employers?" Arutz Shiva, July 25, 2016.
http://www.israelnationalnews.com/News/News.aspx/215507
[174] https://www.unwatch.org/unga-israel-resolutions-2016/ and
https://www.unwatch.org/wp-content/uploads/2009/12/3rc-Cttee.pdf

would treat you better? And by "treat you better," that also includes not killing you. Is there even a single country where the Arabs who live in Israel (one fifth of their population) have more freedoms elsewhere in the Middle East than in Israel?

Much like the Hamas government which is happy to use their own citizens as human shields, their hatred of Israel (and the Jews) far outweighs their concern for the Palestinians. And of course, Hamas has ushered praise upon BDS.

Though BDS claims to oppose nothing more than Israeli settlements, one must understand that in their view, all of Israel is on occupied land. Just read their founding principles contained in the document "Palestinian Civil Society (PSC) Calls for BDS" and that becomes clear. Near the end of the first paragraph of the 2005 document, it states "Fifty-seven years after the state of Israel was built mainly on land ethnically cleansed of its Palestinian owners, a majority of Palestinians are refugees, most of whom are stateless. Moreover, Israel's entrenched system of racial discrimination against its own Arab-Palestinian citizens remains intact."[175]

So, are we to believe that a movement which erroneously believes Israel was built upon land "ethnically cleansed of its Palestinian owners" only has issue with their settlements? If that were the case, they wouldn't have started their timeline with Israel's founding (57 years prior to the documents publication), but with the 1967 War in which Israel took two territories they still hold (the Golan Heights from Syria, and West Bank from Jordan).

---

[175] "Palestinian Civil Society Call for BDS." BDS Movement, July 9, 2005. https://bdsmovement.net/call

Indeed, they issue three conditions that Israel would have to abide by for their boycotts to be lifted - two of three being completely unrelated to the aftermath of the 1967 Six Day War. Among them are ending their "occupation and colonization of all Arab lands and dismantling the Wall," "recognizing the fundamental rights of the Arab-Palestinian citizens of Israel to full equality," and "respecting, protesting, and promoting the rights of Palestinian refugees to return to their homes and properties."

The last two demands have nothing to do with the 1967 war - and the third demand would require Israel to grant citizenship to over 5 million Palestinians, 77 percent of which (or 89 percent, depending on what poll you look at)[176] support Hamas' rocket attacks against Israel, and 80 percent of which support attempts by "individual Palestinians to stab or run over Israelis in Jerusalem and the rest of the West Bank."[177] And that "Wall" referenced in the first demand is the Israeli West Bank Barrier - which was constructed during the second intifada, greatly reducing the frequency of suicide bombings.

This mirrors the stance of Hamas and the Palestinian Authority - that all of Israel is merely "occupied Palestine."

---

[176] Kredo, Adam. "Poll: 89 Percent of Palestinians Support Terror Attacks on Israel." The Washington Free Beacon, August 27, 2014. http://freebeacon.com/national-security/poll-89-percent-of-palestinians-support-terror-attacks-on-israel

[177] "Poll: Huge Majority of Palestinians Support Terror Against Israeli Civilians." The Algemeiner, December 10, 2014. http://www.algemeiner.com/2014/12/10/poll-huge-majority-of-palestinians-support-terror-against-israeli-civilians/

Additionally, we can look no further than what prominent BDS activists have revealed in their own words as to their true intentions.

- BDS co-founder Omar Barghouti opposes the two-state solution, and has stated that "Israel "was Palestine, and there is no reason why it should not be renamed Palestine."[178] More importantly, he's informed us that his calls for boycott would continue even if Israel withdrew from all their settlements, because "The majority of the Palestinian people are not suffering from occupation, they are suffering from denial of their right to come back home."

- According to Palestinian-American legal scholar Noura Erakat, it was understood by the NGOs that signed onto the PSC's aforementioned document "viewed the comprehensive approach to Palestinian rights as a veiled endorsement of the one-state solution."[179]

- Ahmed Moor, a Palestinian-American anti-Israel commenter stated that he "view[s] the BDS movement as a long-term project with radically transformative potential.... BDS is not another step on the way to the final showdown; BDS is The Final Showdown...This belief grows directly from the conviction that nothing resembling the "two-state solution" will ever come into being. Ending the

---

[178] Omar Barghouti, The New Intifada: Resisting Infidel's Apartheid. P. 176
[179] Lim, Audrea, ed. The Case for Sanctions against Israel. London: Verso, 2012. Pp. 88-89.

occupation doesn't mean anything if it doesn't mean upending the Jewish state itself."[180]

But back to Hamas.

After ushering praise upon BDS, Hamas spokesman Izzat al-Risheq bemoaned the opposition the movement faces in America. "The attempts by the U.S. Administration to prevent the rise of the political, economic and academic boycott against Israel makes it complicit in the crimes and terror against the Palestinian people."[181]

He then added "We call for escalating the campaign to isolate the occupation and end the existence of its usurper entity." The "end the existence of its usurper entity" comment is a call to eliminate Israel - just as the Hamas charter spells out.[182]

---

[180] Diker, Dan. "Unmasking BDS: Radical Roots, Extremist Ends." The Israel Group, February 2015. https://theisraelgroup.org/wp-content/uploads/2015/02/Unmasking-BDS.pdf
[181] Toameh, Khaled Abu. "BDS and Hamas: The New Partnership." The Gatestone Institute, June 12, 2015.
https://www.gatestoneinstitute.org/5940/bds-hamas
[182] In the words of Abraham Foxman of the Anti-Defamation league, the charter "reads like a modern-day Mein Kampf," repeating the usual antisemetic conspiracies about Jewish control of the media, being responsible for history's wars, and plenty of other nonense.
Prior to the introduction of the 1988 Hamas Covenant is a quote from Muslim Brotherhood founder Imam Hassan al-Banna: "Israel will exist and will continue to exist until Islam will obliterate it, just as it obliterated others before it." Article seven of the covenant quotes Mohammad having stated that "The Day of Judgement will not come about until Moslems fight the Jews (killing the Jews), when the Jew will hide behind stones and trees. The stones and trees will say O Moslems, O Abdulla, there is a Jew behind me, come and kill him. Only the Gharkad tree, (evidently a certain kind of tree) would not do that because it is one of the trees of the Jews."

And Hamas is hardly the only radical group complementing BDS. In late November, the BDS National Committee published a position paper titled "United Against Apartheid, Colonialism, and Occupation: Dignity & Justice for the Palestinian People," and named 95 organizers that had signed on and endorsed the document.

Among the other endorsers is the Swiss-based "Alkarama for Human Rights," a financer of al-Qaeda who's had a number of their members classified as "specially designated global terrorists" by the U.S. treasury in December 2013.

The top-listed signatory is the Council of National and Islamic Forces in Palestine (CNIF), which consists of a number of organizations, many of which have been designated as terrorist organizations. These include the Islamic Jihad Movement in Palestine, and the Popular Front for the Liberation of Palestine.

BDS is a despicable movement that only one who hates Israel more than they care for the Palestinians could ever support. Even notorious anti-Israel scholars like Norman Finkelstein describe BDS as a "cult," who has views "inconsistent with international law's recognition of Israel's existence."[183] Naturally, the man who built his entire career out of criticism of Israel expressing disdain for an organization as fanatical as BDS led to him being branded a "zionist bully," "angry right-wing pundit" (he's a socialist), and "someone who opposes rights for all Palestinians."

---

[183] Smith, Jordan Michael. "An Unpopular Man." The New Republic, July 7, 2015. https://newrepublic.com/article/122257/unpopular-man-norman-finkelstein-comes-out-against-bds-movement

Hopefully those backing BDS will be more consistent in their support of terrorism, and openly declare their support for al-Qaeda or ISIS next.

CHAPTER NINE
Qur'an vs. The Constitution

I wanted to conclude the book with an outline of how the Qur'an's values conflict with western culture, particularly in showing their conflict with western law. While Jack focused on the Qur'an's conflict with the Magna Carta, I on the other side of the Atlantic will be focusing on how the Qur'an conflicts with the Constitution. This chapter should also serve as a useful reference for those needing ammunition in a debate with someone clueless about what the Qur'an actually says.

Freedom of Religion

It's a common misconception that the reference to a "separation of church and state" comes from the first amendment. The First Amendment doesn't mention that phrase, and rather, reads "Congress shall make no law respecting an establishment of religion, or prohibiting the free exercise thereof; or abridging the freedom of speech, or of the press; or the right of the people peaceably to assemble, and to petition the Government for a redress of grievances."

But separation of church and state is indeed a value the constitution does enforce, even without mentioning the phrase. The actual reference to separation of church of state comes from an 1802 letter that President Thomas Jefferson wrote to the Danbury Baptists. The context is interesting - because it was a religious institution wanting a separation of church and state. The relevant portion of his letter reads:

Believing with you that religion is a matter which lies solely between Man & his God, that he owes account to none other for his faith or his worship, that the legitimate powers of government reach actions only, & not opinions, I contemplate with sovereign reverence that act of the whole American people which declared that their legislature should "make no law respecting an establishment of religion, or prohibiting the free exercise thereof," thus building a wall of separation between Church & State.[184]

That's quite the opposite of what we see in the Muslim world.

As previously documented, punishment for apostasy is widely practiced (and supported) in the Muslim world. The verse mandating death of apostasy can be found in the Hadith, Sahih Bukhari (52:260), "...The Prophet said, 'If somebody (a Muslim) discards his religion, kill him.'"

Jews and Christians at least get the luxury of being able to live in states ruled by Islam, but not without paying a tax called Jizya. When the alternative is death, that sounds like a pretty good deal. Now, just imagine for a second the kind of response you'd see from the Left if President Donald Trump attempted to put a special tax on Muslims - and threaten to kill them if they don't obey. That's exactly what Qur'an 9:29 makes policy, stating "Fight those of the People of the Book who do not truly believe in God and the Last Day, who do not forbid what God and His Messenger have forbidden, who do not obey the rule of justice, until they pay the tax promptly and agree to submit."

Indeed, it's clear that the purpose of Jizya is to purposely force non-Muslims to live as second class citizens. In verses prior to the one outlining the Jizya, the Qur'an encourages Muslims not to befriend non-believers, even if

---

[184] Jefferson, Thomas. "Jefferson's Letter to the Danbury Baptists (January 1st, 1802)." Library of Congress, https://www.loc.gov/loc/lcib/9806/danpre.html

they're family. Qur'an 9:23 commands "Believers, do not take your fathers and brothers as allies if they prefer disbelief to faith: those of you who do so are doing wrong."

Luckily, actual enforcement of the Jizya largely disappeared from the Muslim world during the 20th century, though it's been revived in territory held by groups like ISIS, al-Qaeda, the Taliban, and others.

Freedom of Speech & Freedom of Dissent

Freedom to speech naturally includes the freedom to criticize religion, and is protected by the first amendment. Not so in Islam - as you've likely gleaned from statistics cited earlier showing the Muslim world's attitude toward blasphemy.

The offending verses are as follows:

- Qur'an 4:140: "As He has already revealed to you [believers] in the Scripture, if you hear people denying and ridiculing God's revelation, do not sit with them unless they start to talk of other things, or else you will become like them. God will gather all the hypocrites and disbelievers together in hell."

- Qur'an 28:55: "...and turn away whenever they hear frivolous talk, saying 'We have our deeds and you have yours. Peace be with you! We do not seek the company of foolish people.'"

- Qur'an 9:47: ". . . But they uttered blasphemy . . . if they repent, it will be best for them, but if they turn back, Allah will punish them."

As for the punishment, turn to the Hadiths and in Sunan Abu Dawood 38:4349 we learn that "A Jewess used to abuse the Prophet and disparage him. A man strangled her till she died. The Apostle of Allah declared that no recompense was payable for her blood."

Of course, practically all religions prohibit blasphemy (and the same kind of death penalty for blasphemy can be found in the Book of Leviticus, 24:16),[185] but nowhere more is punishment for it enforced than in Muslim countries. Below is pictured the nations that still have blasphemy laws in effect, with nearly all being Muslim-majority. The only nations where death is the sentence for blasphemy are Muslim countries.[186]

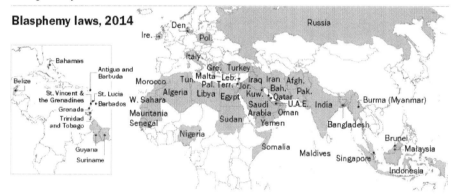

Blasphemy laws, 2014

Note: Countries with a blasphemy law, rule or policy at some level of government during calendar year 2014.
Source: Pew Research Center analysis.

PEW RESEARCH CENTER

When it comes to punishing apostasy, all but India are Muslim-majority nations.

---

[185] Though Christians at least enjoy the luxury of being able to point out that Jesus abolished the law of Moses.
[186] Theodorou, Angelina E. "Which countries still outlaw apostasy and blasphemy?" Pew Research Center, July 29, 2016.
http://www.pewresearch.org/fact-tank/2016/07/29/which-countries-still-outlaw-apostasy-and-blasphemy/

Apostasy laws, 2014

Note: Countries with an apostasy law, rule or policy at some level of government during calendar year 2014.
Source: Pew Research Center analysis.

PEW RESEARCH CENTER

Cruel and Unusual Punishment

The eighth amendment to the Bill of Rights grants protection against cruel and unusual punishment, stating that "Excessive bail shall not be required, nor excessive fines imposed, nor cruel and unusual punishments inflicted."

As you're all aware from the polling from Pew earlier in this book, support for the barbaric punishment the Qur'an is known for (stonings, amputations, etc) are widely supported in the Muslim world. And of course they are - as the Qur'an commands them. Below is a brief directory...

- Cutting off the hands of thieves, Qur'an 5:38 - "Cut off the hands of thieves, whether there are man or woman, as punishment for what they have done - a deterrent from God: God is almighty and wise."

192

- Crucify, amputate, banish, or kill those who fight Islam, Qur'an 5:33-34 - "Those who wage war against God and His Messenger and strive to spread corruption in the land should be punished by death, crucifixion, the amputation of an alternate hand and foot, or punishment from the land: a disgrace for them in this world, and then a terrible punishment in the thereafter."

- Confine "lewd" women to the home until they're dead, Qur'an 4:15 - "If any of your women commit a lewd act, call four witnesses from among you, then, if they testify to their guilt, keep the woman at home until death comes to them or until God shows them another way." Men caught committing lewd acts receive an unspecified punishment, and if they repent, they can be left alone.

- Beatings for drinking alcohol, Bukhari 8.81: "Abu Huraira said, 'A man who drank wine was brought to the Prophet. The Prophet said, "Beat him!" Abu Huraira added, "So some of us beat him with our hands, and some with their shoes, and some with their garments (by twisting it) like a lash, and then when we finished, someone said to him, 'May Allah disgrace you!' On that the Prophet said, 'Do not say so, for you are helping Satan to overpower him.'"

- An eye for an eye leaves the world Islamic, Qur'an 5:45: "In the Torah We prescribed for them a life for a life, an eye for an eye, a nose for a nose, and ear for an ear, a tooth for a tooth, an equal wound for a wound: if anyone forgoes this out of charity, it will serve as atonement for his bad deeds. Those who do

193

not judge according to what God has revealed are doing grave wrong."

- Death to homosexuals, Abu Dawud (4462): "The Messenger of Allah (peace and blessings of Allah be upon him) said, "Whoever you find doing the action of the people of Lot, execute the one who does it and the one to whom it is done." The "people of Lot" are making a reference to the story of Sodom and Gomorrah in the Old Testament.

The Qur'an makes reference to the story of Sodom and Gomorrah in the seventh book, going out of the way to distinguish homosexuality from other sins. Verses 7:80-84 states: "We sent Lot and he said to his people, 'How can you practice this outrage? No other people has done so before. You lust after men rather than women! You transgress all bounds! The only response his people gave was to say, 'drive them out of your town! These men want to keep themselves chaste!' We saved him and his kinsfolk-apart from his wife who stayed behind - and We showered upon the rest of them a rain of destruction. See the fate of the evildoers."

Equal Protection Under the Law

The equal protection clause of the Constitution's 14th amendment grants the right to equal protection under the laws - while the Qur'an mandates a system of Muslim superiority in the law, but male supremacy above all.

Among the more commonly known verses giving Muslim men more rights than women comes from Qur'an verse 2:282, we learn that the testimony of a woman is only worth half that of a man's. "Call in two men as witnesses. If two men are not there, then call one man and two women out of those who approve you as witnesses, so that if one of the two women should forget, the other can remind her."

The"forgetfulness" of women is hardly mentioned only once in Islam's holy texts. The hadiths are a tad more explicit in why the testimony of women are only worth one half of a man's. Here's Sahih Burkari: 1:6:301:

> Once Allah's Apostle went out to the Musalla (to offer the prayer) o 'Id-al-Adha or Al-Fitr prayer. Then he passed by the women and said, "O women! Give alms, as I have seen that the majority of the dwellers of Hell-fire were you (women)." They asked, "Why is it so, O Allah's Apostle ?" He replied, **"You curse frequently and are ungrateful to your husbands. I have not seen anyone more deficient in intelligence and religion than you. A cautious sensible man could be led astray by some of you."** The women asked, **"O Allah's Apostle! What is deficient in our intelligence and religion?" He said, "Is not the evidence of two women equal to the witness of one man?" They replied in the affirmative. He said, "This is the deficiency in her intelligence. Isn't it true that a woman can neither pray nor fast during her menses?" The women replied in the affirmative.** He said, "This is the deficiency in her religion."

Perhaps these supposed mental deficiencies are partially responsible for the majority of those in hell being women, as "The Prophet said: 'I was shown the Hell-fire and that the majority of its dwellers were women who were ungrateful.' It was asked, 'Do they disbelieve in Allah'" (or are they ungrateful to Allah?) He replied, "They are ungrateful to their husbands and are ungrateful for the favors and the good (charitable deeds) done to them" (al-Bukhari: 1:2:29).

Back to women's treatment under Islamic law - women being worth "one-half" that of a man is a common theme. We can glean from the fourth chapter of the Qur'an, titled "Woman" that "a son should have the equivalent share of two daughters [in inheritance] (verse 11), and it doesn't stop there.

Suppose for instance, someone dies childless - but has a single sister. Verse 176 has that covered - "if a man leaves one sister, she is entitled to half the inheritance." Who gets the other half? God knows (and didn't reveal it in the Qur'an). If there are no children left behind, but a sister and a brother, the brother is entitled to two-thirds of the inheritance.

Moving on from inheritance, let's talk about another phenomenon involving the splitting up of assets: divorce. There's no shortage of evidence that the divorce courts favor women in America (in terms of alimony granted, percentage of times it's the mother granted custody of the children, among other areas) - but that's preferable any day of the week to divorce under Islamic law.

In taking "no fault divorce" laws to a whole new level, the sharia allows a husband to divorce his wife merely by stating "you are divorced" three times in the presence of two males (but not even four women). Bizarrely, if the man regrets his decision and wants to remarry his wife, she must first marry another man who will then repudiate her (Qur'an 2:229-30). Of course, women are not afforded such power.

Female Leadership

Following backlash to the Trump presidency, USA Today ran a story headlined "Hijab becomes symbol of resistance, feminism in age of Trump." In another century, perhaps similarly-minded people will allow the confederate flag to become a symbol of opposition to racism - which would make just as much sense.

These protestors believe themselves to be "intersectional," showing solidarity with two groups that they believe to be targets of the Trump administration (Muslims, and women). For all the complaining that misogyny is to blame for Hillary Clinton's defeat - the odds of her running in the first place would've been closer to zero in a country where women are mandated to wear the hijab.

In Sahih Bukhari 92:50, Muhammad hears the news that the Persians had made the daughter of Khosrau their queen - news to which Muhammad reacted by responding "Never will succeed such a nation as makes a woman their ruler." Well, if that woman's name is "Hillary Clinton" he may have a point.

Among the defenses of the verse is that Muhammad was speaking specifically of Persia, but the wording of "such a nation" clearly makes such an interpretation unlikely.

While it's not like there's anything in the Constitution explicitly mentioning female leadership, the Constitution does grant everyone the right to life, liberty, and the pursuit of happiness. The word "Islam" itself means submission, and when one reads the Qur'an, it becomes clear that the religion leaves no room for human freedom. Everything is owed to God - simply for the sake of being owed to God.

At the heart of Western civilization is individualism. No intellectual tradition outside of Western philosophy has been as preoccupied with the concept of the "individual" - and the rights that must come along with it. We are free to pursue whatever we desire (as long as it doesn't impose harm on others), think whatever we want, and pursue whatever business interests we desire (which I mention only because of the Qur'an's prohibition on charging interest).

By stark contrast, the Qur'an's philosophy is collectivist to its core, and the consequences can be seen simply by looking at the fruits of the societies it's built. Even while in economic ruin, Greece (with a population under 11 million) translates five times as many books into Greek every year than the entire Muslim world translates into Arabic. If that wasn't shocking enough, there are more books translated into Spanish every year than have been translated in Arabic in the past 1000 years.[187]

Despite the scientific accomplishments made during the Islamic Golden Age, they ended there. With a population of 1.6 billion (meaning slightly over 1 in 5 people on Earth are Muslim), only two adherents of the religion have won a Nobel prize in the sciences. Meanwhile, Jews, who number only 12 million (or fewer than 2 out of every 1,000 people) have won 141 Nobel's in the sciences - or 171 if you count "the dismal science."[188]

---

[187] Harris, David. "Three Middle East Myths Exploded." The Huffington Post. http://www.huffingtonpost.com/david-harris/three-middle-east-myths-e_b_821537.html
[188] See: Lists of Nobel Laureates by Religion. https://en.wikipedia.org/wiki/Category:Lists_of_Nobel_laureates_by_r eligion

One need only look up photographs of Afghanistan before Taliban rule, or Iran prior to the Islamic revolution to see that cultural repression, and the consequences of it, are by design. The direct consequences of Islam's barbarism (mainly from the punishments mandated by the Sharia) are easy for one to see and express disgust over, but the cumulative effects Islam has on eroding a culture that embraces individuality and freedom tends to generate much less outrage from the Left.

49767440R00115

Made in the USA
San Bernardino, CA
04 June 2017